'Habbie' to 'Jeely Eater'

IAN MILLER

AN AUTOBIOGRAPHY

Published by Neetah Books
www.neetahbooks.com
First printing: May 2016
Copyright (c) 2016 by Ian Miller. All rights reserved.

Printed by Ingram.

All photographs are courtesy of Ian Miller.

A CIP catalogue for this title is available from the British Library.

ISBN: 978-1-908898-22-7

This book is also available in Kindle.

DEDICATION

Dedicated to my wife Joan, my best friend who has been tolerant of my idiosyncrasies, supportive of my commitment to church and community and understanding of my "view" of retirement. In short, who has allowed and enabled me to be the fellow I am. It is a debt I can never repay.

To my greatly loved son's Derek and Andrew of whom I am immensely proud. They are everything I hoped they would be and of course their choice of "perfect" wives Natalie and Andrea... whom I regard as my daughters as well. I am also indebted to them for providing Joan and I with the greatest gift of all ...our grandchildren Ben, Josh, Rowan and Jake. They make our life complete.

ACKNOWLEDGEMENTS

To Willie Scobie... who inspired, cajoled, bullied and eventually convinced me to write this book.

To Paul Murdoch who graciously agreed to publish it and make what started as a "vanity" into a reality and whose ideas, commitment and enthusiasm made me believe that it would be read!

To Alice McWilliam, who corrected many of the typos, spelling and grammar. Alice was my former secretary at Bonhill Church also a friend whose support could always be relied and whose laughter and humour made any dreary day bearable.

To Douglas Campbell, a journalist and Derek's, father in law who brought his professional expertise to my task and whose kindly advice was both acceptable and invaluable.

To Bill Heaney and Keith Charters for their advice, expertise and hard work during the final stages of this book.

To the village of Kilbarchan.... a wonderful place to grow up! A place that provided me with so many happy memories and sometimes memories that cannot be shared for fear of "repercussion".

To Bonhill and the wider Vale of Leven who have been warm and accepting to me and mine. The best of all places to live who refused to have me on a pedestal and who have paid me the greatest honour of regarding me as "Ian"... their friend.

To My parents Ernie and Beatrice who encouraged, supported, affirmed me... and loved me. They could not have done more for their only and sometimes" spoiled" son, who also with Willie and Lizzie Parr made the same "Habbie to Jeely Eater" journey.

To our lifelong friends from Kilbarchan whose company we still enjoy.

To our friends in the Vale, too numerous to mention but whose friendship we will never take for granted.

To the Church in Bonhill.... the members and office bearers of this unique congregation. I believe we were made for each other and hope they feel likewise.

To all those who have made my life what it has been, especially to those whose lives I have shared at happy and sad times, to those whose names appear, and to those unnamed who were also part of the story and of my life.

SPONSORS

A huge thank you to all the sponsors listed below.

Sean and Anna Brady
Joanne Brannigan
Stewart and Linda Brown
Stewart (Jnr) Rebekah and Rory and Stewart Brown.
Steven, Holly (nee Brown) and Innis Button
Mr and Mrs Alan Cawley
The Crawford Family
John and Aileen Daly
Ella and Bill Davidson
Robert Dawson
Iain and Sheila Galbraith
Gordon and Isobel Glen
David and Lisa Glen
John and Maureen Kane
Stuart and Nieve King
Jessie Macdonald
Jim and Mary McGlashan
Malcolm, Shiona and Kirsty Mackay
Sheila and Duncan Mckinlay
Moira and Jim McLean
Sheila and Ken MacLeod
Murdo and Mhairi Macleod
Eddie and Dorothy McMurray.
Ronald and Colina McQueen
Alice, Alan and Gavin McWilliam
Andrew and Andrea Miller
Rowan Miller
Jake Miller
Derek and Natalie Miller
Ben Miller
Josh Miller
Jeanette and Willie Murray
Billy and Mary Nimmo

Irene and Isaac Owens
Dorothy Paterson
Jean (the giggler) and Robert Percival
Irene Watt
Irene Watson
The Wright Family Drymen

Alexandria and Dumbarton Funeral Care
Cawley Hotels, Duck Bay, Loch Lomond.
The Cruin, Arden, Loch Lomond
Tommy and Petra McMillan The Dumbuck Hotel
The Fountain Tavern
John H Glen Funeral Undertaker
Great Start Childcare
Horizon Security Solutions
John Kane Funeral Director
McKenzies Bar
Mei Beauty
Rogers Skip Hire
The Stables Balloch
Wright Taxis

In memory of our fantastic Husband and Dad…Bobby - (the Cawley Family)
In memory of my parents…Jackie and Peggy Burch - (Mrs Margaret Cawley)
In memory of Rose Cawley - (the Cawley Family)
In memory of George Adam - (Mrs Kathleen Adams and family)
In memory of Ian Dalglish Graham – (from his family)
In Memory of John and Margaret Galbraith, beloved parents of Iain Galbraith
In Memory of the Galbraith family of Old Bonhill who served the Bonhill Kirk so well in their day
In memory of Donald Macdonald - (Jessie and family)
In memory of John H and Sarah Glen - (The Glen Family)

PROLOGUE

HER Majesty smiled as we made our way through the Balmoral estate in the Range Rover. We were bound for a barbecue and the Queen, Elizabeth II no less, was something of an expert on those unmade roads. I just enjoyed the scenery and the chat. If my Mum and Dad could have seen me then. Wow.

It was rather difficult not to pinch myself as the vehicle trundled through this beautiful part of the countryside. Here I was, Ian Hunter Miller, minister of Bonhill Church in the lovely Vale of Leven, being chauffeured by our monarch on a bright summer evening.

I know my mother, Beatrice Hunter, was rather keen for her only child to make something of himself. All parents hope and pray this will be the case with their offspring. However, Balmoral? The Queen? This scenario would be best left to the authors of children's fantasy. However, there I was, bumping along and sharing a conversation with one of best-known women on earth. I was thrilled and hoped Her Majesty was enjoying the company.

After taking the service as a guest preacher at Crathie Church, I returned to the Castle for a spot of light lunch, at which all the royals were there, Prince Phillip, Charles, Camilla, Edward and his wife Sophie. Andrew and his daughters, Beatrice and Eugenie, were there too. They were just like any other family on holiday, relaxed and at ease. They were also both charming and welcoming.

When the weekend was over, Richard, my *chauffeur*, stood beside the gleaming black Co-operative limo, which was kindly provided and made ready to whisk me back to reality. What an experience. Maybe it was something for the Queen to cherish and tell her great grandchildren about, but most probably not. However, it was certainly something for me to cherish and to tell mine.

In my life and work, I was sometimes forthright and impatient. I have never been slow to act when I felt doing something immediately was what was needed. There have been situations, however, where, with hindsight, I should have taken a step back and where I have said things when it probably would have been better to remain tight-lipped.

Many years before, however, saying nothing was not an option when I first met a pretty young lass who turned up at a Youth Fellowship meeting in Kilbarchan. Later, I was to discover she had come along, not because she had been seeking spiritual truth, but because it was the only way her mother would allow her to go out on a Sunday night in her Sunday best. I must have done and said something right because when I popped the question, Joan Parr said 'yes' and now, 47 years later, we remain blissfully married, with two great sons and four fabulous grandchildren. God has been good to me.

On the subject of children, having worked in the Vale all of my ministerial life, I still get great pleasure from performing the marriage ceremony of youngsters I baptised all those years before. Then, in turn, when they decide to have a family, the process starts all over again. I have also been privileged to officiate at the marriage of many rich the famous people, with as many footballers from Celtic and Rangers saying, 'I do,' in front of me as would make up the line-up for several good teams.

Of course, alongside every joyous moment, a parish minister is called upon to lighten the load of the bereaved in their darkest hour. You can be smiling one minute after having welcomed an infant into the Church, or joining a couple in matrimony, and the next saying words of comfort to people as a close friend or family member is laid to rest.

When injustice, discrimination or perceived unfairness has raised its ugly head, I have seldom been backward at coming forward.

I have had many a difference of opinion with the Health Board over the years regarding health provision at our local hospital. When a place on the Board was offered to me, it was something I was happy to accept.

Better to be inside fighting whatever battle came along than outside treading water.

Perhaps the biggest battle I have fought would relate to nuclear weapons. My opposition has been lifelong and total. I have never deviated from the opinion that they are an incomprehensible obscenity and a repugnant waste of money. Some of the population barely manage to make ends meet, while the United Kingdom government seem happy and content to hand over £billions for weapons we will never use. This is absurd.

I think – I hope - that my Mum and Dad would be reasonably satisfied with how their son turned out, speaking up when needed, while staying silent when necessary, although Joan may question that from time to time.

The time came for me to retire in June 2012, although the truth is I seem to be working more hours than ever since leaving Bonhill Church. I have been privileged since retirement to have been involved in many churches in our area and continue to work at Luss and Arrochar Parish Churches. I am repeatedly told by my family to slow down but perhaps I do suffer from selective deafness.

It all kicked-off for me on the other side of the River Clyde, in the Renfrewshire village of Kilbarchan ...

CHAPTER ONE

EARLY LIFE

EVEN before I had glimpsed the light of day or taken my first breath, I was impatient. So impatient, in fact, that I made my presence felt before my mother even reached Johnstone Maternity Hospital. Try as I might, I have never quite mastered that wonderful quality of patience that I so admire in others. Fairly soon after my premature entrance into this world, I made my way back, with my parents, Ernie and Beatrice, to 5 Low Barholm, Kilbarchan, which was to be my home for the next 25 years.

My childhood was happy. More than happy. You take things for granted as a child. Subconsciously, I suppose, I just accepted that I was the centre of the universe. As an only child, with no rivals on the way, nor indeed wanted, life was good and I felt loved. I took it for granted that every mum and dad was like my mum and dad. Later, I was to realise that was not the case.

As I've reflected on my childhood, my admiration for my father has grown. I was in my teens when I discovered his romantic links with my mum had been discouraged. Though both were from the East End of Greenock, my dad, Ernie, was the youngest son from a large and close family all deeply involved in the Christian Brethren. Ernie had lost his Dad when he was still a boy and life could not have been easy for the family. Work was scarce and to supplement the family income, he and his elder brother Bert, used to buy fish from the fish market to sell around the large houses of rural Renfrewshire. Ernie eventually won an apprenticeship at John G Kincaid, Marine engineers in Greenock and that brought to an end a partnership that might have rivalled Del Boy and Rodney.

My mum, Beatrice, was to all intent and purposes, an only child. She had a younger brother but he died in infancy. She was set for a career in music and was accepted for the Royal Academy in Glasgow. Ernie remembers her as a 'wee lassie with pigtails' playing the piano at Greenock High School as the children marched into morning assembly.

Gran Hunter, (Beatrice's mother) felt Beatrice could do better than marry an engineer and should initially complete her studies at the Academy and enter the teaching profession. Beatrice and her mother Bridget (an interesting name for someone with decidedly Orange leanings), had one thing in common...a very determined nature. Beatrice was in love with Ernie Miller and no one was going to change that. Rather sadly, in view of the parental opposition, Beatrice was forced to leave home but her future mother in law ensured there was a roof over her head. Rather interestingly her father John Hunter, who was the manager of the local Galbraith's food store, was very fond of Ernie, and Beatrice's grandfather, Sam Connolly, even more so. However, Bridget, like another strong-willed woman of a later era, was not for turning. There was an impasse.

In due course they did marry in the Co-operative hall in Greenock. Shortly afterwards they moved to Kilbarchan and set up residence in a room and kitchen. It was to this home that I was to return after my rather hurried entry into this world at the Thorn Maternity Hospital in Johnstone on the 30th May 1944.

This was a family divide, which showed no signs of healing. There is little doubt that Ernie Miller's skill as a peacemaker and diplomat knew no bounds. In an incredibly gracious act, (knowing he was far from being the favoured one), he took his weeks-old child on the bus down to Greenock. He climbed the stairs of the tenement flat in Ratho Street and knocked the door. Gran answered. Before she could say a word, Ernie handed her a bundle and said, 'This is your grandson.'

This simple act broke the ice. The family was re-united and I was never aware of anything other than the obvious fact that John and Beasy (Bridget) Hunter loved Ernie Miller. In fact, in their later years, having to choose between their daughter and their son in law, I feel sure they would have chosen the latter.

I have witnessed acrimonious family disputes. I have seen it at weddings and funerals where the hatred has been palpable.

There is little doubt that my mother had me on the highest pedestal. My wife Joan used to say, 'Ian, if you robbed a bank your Mum would say... 'Och aye but oor Ian must have known someone was in need.' In all of the scrapes and escapades as a schoolboy and teenager, Mum hid my misdemeanours and I was always sure of her unconditional love.

Sadly, shortly after I was born, she developed rheumatoid arthritis, which limited her musical ability. I do, however, have many memories of Dad and her playing the piano together. They were both musical, but arthritis certainly put paid to her career in music. This affliction she bore with fortitude and never once did I hear her complain, even when she was struggling to comb my hair, as a five-year-old child, on my way to Kilbarchan Primary School.

I have memories of the school and of all its teachers, Miss Leggat, Miss Calder, Miss Miller, Miss Stewart, Mrs Gray, Mrs Kennedy, Mr McArthur and Miss Anderson (Wee Puggy... Don't ask me why). The heidie was Mr Wallace, later replaced by Stanley Chadwin. I often seemed to be in trouble, being belted or sent to the heidie. My main ambition was to be the class clown, and that has never quite left me.

My grandparents, John and Beasy Hunter, left Greenock and moved to Locher Terrace in Bridge of Weir to be near us. How things change. I remember sitting on my grandfather's knee and he would read to me, by the light of a flickering paraffin lamp, a book entitled String Lug the Fox by David Stephen. There was no electricity at Locher Terrace in the 1950s. Those moments live on in my memory. It was a place where I felt safe and greatly loved. My grandparents were later to move to Easwald Drive, Kilbarchan, with all the marvels of both electricity and gas. In some ways, I became the centre of their lives. I was their only grandchild and spoiled.

My other grandmother, Eleanor Miller had, by contrast, nine grandchildren. She had the wonderful ability of treating each one as if they were the only one. She lived with my maiden aunt Nora who was everyone's favourite. She was great fun to be with and nothing was ever too much trouble. I have met a few 'saints' in my life and the unique thing is that real saints never know it. I have met even more who thought they were saints and were, almost without exception, as far from sainthood as it is possible to be. Aunt Nora was the real thing. She and granny Miller also moved to Kilbarchan.

Summer was idyllic for me. I spent a huge amount of time with the Blair family at Cartside Farm. Hugh Blair had endless time and patience with me. I spent hours at the farm, jumping in the hay loft, travelling on the horse drawn, flat bedded trailer which brought the hay-ricks back to the farm, chasing the mice that scurried from under it, watching with awe - the big black ominous eye of the bull, safely tethered in the byre. We used to wonder why, as children, we were chased away from the byre when the 'bull with the bowler hat' came to call. Later we were to realise it was the vet and that his visit, with his bag of tricks, meant that the bull was missing his usual dalliance with the herd of cows. Maybe that was the reason for his baleful stare.

Kilbarchan had a history although, as a child growing up, I could not have cared less. It was famous for handloom weaving. At one time, there were 800 looms in the village. The weavers were active politically and sought the reform of parliament. It would be fair to say they were politically well to the left of centre. I am not sure if that strong leftish leaning continues in the village, but weaving does, with demonstrations being given at the Weavers Cottage, owned by the National Trust.

Towards the end of primary school, when parental influences were relaxed, and after the compulsory homework, I would be allowed out. Even on a dark winter's night. I think there was a curfew of 8.00pm on weeknights and 9.00pm at weekends. I confess now that along with some of my school friends we would play 'ring bang scoosh', ringing the bells of Kilbarchan's many residences and then running away, vaulting hedges, putting out the gas lights at Kilbarchan railway station and incurring the wrath of station master, Albert Haynes. On summer evenings, it was 'spoolying' (stealing) apples from the larger Kilbarchan gardens. Of such anti-social activity, my parents were blissfully unaware.

Kilbarchan was a good place to grow up. Sledging in the public park during winter, then football and cricket in the summer when days seemed long and endless. We played in the Glentyan Estate or the Grove Estate with one watchful eye looking out for the 'gamie' (gamekeeper) or the 'dug'. None of these estates had gamekeepers. The Grove estate had a female caretaker who also had a 'dug', large and very hairy (the dug that is). In our minds, it was elevated to Baskerville proportions. It had red, fiery eyes, and must have salivated at the thought of sinking its teeth into the nether regions of errant schoolboys as they escaped over the wall. It had the speed of a greyhound, the strength of a German Shepherd and the tenacity of a Bulldog. In reality, it had none of these. The image of it is fixed in my mind. I now see it as having eaten the crumbs of too many pies that may have fallen from its mistress's table. Frankly, its elderly arthritic owner would have had more chance of catching us, but the legend remained.

Another story related to 'Wallace's Cave', which was situated just over the Milliken wall which bordered the public park. As children, we were warned not to go over the Milliken. That was tantamount to an invitation! It was particularly dubious for a girl to be seen going over there. If seen, her moral reputation would be diminished. May I say that despite this threat many did. The legend was that an underground passage linked the cave to a similar opening in Elderslie (birthplace of William Wallace). Within the school community of Kilbarchan, many claimed to have made that journey. It was all hokum, of course. There was a small opening and perhaps Houdini in his younger years might just have made it. However, we believed just as much as we believed that all the Nans, Annes, Helens, Joans and Alisons, who ventured over the Milliken Wall, did not return with their virtuous reputation intact. Legends have always been part of growing up.

All of this time, along with my parents, I attended the local Brethren Assembly or Mission Hall while still living in the room and kitchen at 5 Low Barholm. There was one drawback. Room and kitchens in the late forties and early fifties were, as they say, 'without facilities'. It certainly taught you to control your bladder and like a camel, go for long distances without the need of water or at least of passing it. I do, however, remember the odd occasion when a dash to the loo on a cold winter's night was necessary. I remember the smell of the paraffin lamp, always kept alight to stop the pipes from freezing and the accumulation of damp editions of yesterday's Daily Record or Bulletin. These were the days before Andrex. It probably made the loo visits more interesting, especially when you chanced upon an edition of the Sunday Post and were able to follow the exploits of Oor Willie or the Broons.

If there was a drawback there was also a plus to living at 5 Low Barholm, for downstairs in a converted weaving shop resided Alex and Charlotte Lightbody. I adopted them as aunt and uncle. They had no choice in the matter and their house soon became my second home. It also acted as a 'city of refuge' when I was in trouble upstairs. Uncle Alex and Aunt Charlotte became big in my life.

Every Saturday Alex would take a bath in the 'washhoose'. Living with Charlotte and his two daughters Betty and Morag it was probably an escape for him, a retreat. His wee friend from 'upstairs' who sat faithfully outside the 'washhoose' door while he was having his ablutions, however, invariably disturbed his reverie.

Occasionally the conversation went like this,

Me, 'Are you in there, Uncle Alex?'

Alex, 'Yes ma chappie.'

Me, 'What are you doing?'

I have always had the ability to ask a question to which there was an obvious answer. The man was having a bath.

Nevertheless, good man that he was, he would humour me and eventually say, 'Are ye listening?' And of course I was, ear pressed against the door. 'I am going to dive into the bath from the 'washhoose biler', he would say and I would listen for the inevitable splashing which ensued and with the mind of the child I could just see this big man faultlessly diving from the elevated position of the boiler into the narrow confines of the zinc bath. If Alex Lightbody said he would do it, I believed him.

He taught me much. He taught me how to jump from an aircraft with a parachute. I figured that one day this might come in handy. He practiced with me jumping from the garden wall and rolling over on the ground when we landed. I got good at it, but eventually tired of the 'make belief' and decided to put my newfound knowledge to the test. Accordingly, I raided the coal cellar and made myself a parachute out of a coal sack (string tied to each of the four corners) and climbed onto the washhouse roof, waiting for my dad to return from work. As he made his way through the close into the back garden I shouted, 'Daddy, watch me,' and leapt off the roof. I plummeted 14 feet and landed with a thump. My Dad dashed up to where I was lying in a heap, then after assuring himself that my injuries were superficial, he intoned, 'Son, yer parachute failed to open.'

At that point, I decided a career with the RAF or civil aviation was not for me. Mind you, it maybe did have a connection when, at a later stage in my life, I was to take up a career where the incumbents are often referred to as 'sky pilots'!

I spent most Saturday evenings with Alex and Charlotte. Alex would head over to Brunetti's ice cream shop, conveniently just across the road, where he would order a liberal quantity of hot peas and vinegar, a portion of ice cream and two bottles of American cream soda. He would take the ice cream and soda and make these amazing iced drinks. All and all, it was, you might say, a lethal digestive combination. During this repast, which we enjoyed with appropriate reverence, he would almost invariably say, 'Man ... this is riotous living.' That phrase stuck with me and he said it often.

The Mission Hall that I attended did not have a designated minister but instead, visiting preachers on a Sunday evening. I think it would be fair to say that there were certain passages of scripture that fascinated those itinerant pastors. One of these was the story of the Prodigal Son as recorded by St Luke. At the 15th chapter, according to Luke, the daft laddie, who left the family home with half the family silver, was a bit of a 'waster' and, in the words of the King James Version of the Bible, 'he wasted his substance on riotous living.' As a child I remember listening to those chaps and wondering, 'what a carry on for an iced drink and a bowl of hot peas'.

However, Alex Lightbody spent time with me. I never remember him buying me a Christmas present or a birthday present but I remember him giving me his time and love. He was a man of true Christian convictions. It was not until later in life that I discovered my Uncle Alex had previously been 'a drunk'. More often than not, he would fail to return home to his wife and two daughters until his wages had been passed over to the barman in their entirety. One day, in Alex's own words, he met Jesus and a miracle occurred. Alex became a living testimony to his faith and a great role model for a growing lad.

Laughter was very much a part of our family life. My Dad was a great joker and full of fun. He would regale us with stories, which I am sure he exaggerated for effect. He returned from work one day to tell us that, at the lunch time break at Kincaid's in Greenock, he and his pal Stanley Barr had got one of the large steel ball bearings used for the Marine Engines. They painted it to look like a rubber ball and rolled it down the road just as some of their workmates were returning to work. Seeing the ball rolling towards them the men dashed en-masse to give it a kick. The lucky fellow who got there first gave it such a wallop that, had it been rubber, it would surely have landed in the Clyde. This story was often re-told. My Mum, a sympathetic soul, used to ask, 'Was the fellow all right?'

'Yes,' Dad would answer, 'Of course he was, but after that his big toe-nail used to grow out of his heel!'

Those were the days when workers did not get holiday pay and put money away weekly into a fund to finance their annual break. It was usual to have one of the workers to act as 'banker'. For some crazy reason Dad was the fund treasurer. He collected the dues every week, presumably banked them and, as the Greenock Fair drew near, he would pay out to the workers what they had entrusted to him. The first Friday of July was payout day. On that day, Dad clocked in and then hid in the factory out of sight. He arranged for a pal to spread the rumour that he had been seen the night before at Cartsdyke station, standing on the platform with a woman, her three children and a whole set of suitcases. According to Dad's pal, it was obvious he had 'done a runner' with the entire holiday fund. The place was in uproar with threats of calling the police. In view of this Dad was alerted to make his appearance. Strangely enough, not everyone saw the funny side of this. He also said, 'They never asked me to take care of the holiday fund again.' I wonder why?

His humour, practical joking and fun made our home very happy. Holidays were important and every year it was either Whitley Bay, Harrogate, The Lake District, or Skye. We would often plan our holiday around a 'Test Match', for Dad was a great cricket fan. I have vivid memories of watching the icons of English cricket.

Primary school passed all too quickly but at the junior school, I found out that even if I did not have the talent to be the dux of the school, my penchant for creating laughter moved me to an even higher level. I must have had some innate intelligence for I was placed in an A class and accordingly studied two languages - French and Latin.

I remember well that, as my time in Johnstone High ended, I had one last Latin exam to face. By this time, Latin and I had very little in common. I could manage *Amo, Amas, Amat ...* and still can, but very little else stuck. As part of the test, I had to translate a passage about Hannibal and a fellow called Eutropius who wrote the Punic Wars. I had very little interest in this Carthaginian and his exploits astride an elephant crossing the Alps.

In 1959 it was the custom for your exam results to be made public and the teacher (in this case Mr Deucher), would shout out the mark achieved by each pupil, starting with the top of the class. And so the names were reeled off Smith - 98 per cent, McWilliam - 94, Shaw - 89, Eadie - 76, Rennie - 68, and so on. I had very little interest at this stage in the proceedings but as the marks dwindled through the sixties and into the fifties, I hoped against hope that my name just might emerge - but no. Barr - 44, Spence - 36, Wylie - 32, Jenkins - 28... On and on, down and down, until there was but one script left... Miller -16 per cent. Mr Deucher held the offending script between his index finger and his thumb and disdainfully let it fall to the ground. I made my way from my seat to retrieve it but he was not finished. 'Miller', he said, 'it's like the prairies.'

'How's that, sir', I said, cocky as always.

'Wide open spaces,' he replied.

And that was pretty much the end of Latin and me.

One other memorable incident remains engraved on my mind. The ability to make folk laugh, even at my own expense, something that has never left me, was a badge of honour but also a character flaw.

During an English lesson, a fellow pupil threw a rubber at me, which bounced off my head and hit another classmate. He reacted with threats of violence. The teacher intervened and whipped me out in front of the class. Suddenly I was being blamed for something I did not do. He was intent on administering the appropriate punishment for such disruptive behaviour. Still protesting my innocence, I refused the punishment. He then removed me from the classroom. As I left, the encouragement of my classmates to continue the defiance was ringing in my ears. Outside the teacher began to reason with me and suggested that if I quietly accepted the punishment that would be the end of it. I was not to be bought off and continued to express innocence. The teacher suddenly whipped out his belt and started lashing me about the body and legs then he turned on his heels and re-entered the classroom. Ten minutes later, he recalled me to the class. By this time, ugly red wealds were beginning to develop on my legs and upper body, which I displayed to all and sundry. I was encouraged by my classmates to tell my father and have him come in the next day to 'stiffen the teacher'.

My Dad was a very mild man (who I do not think ever 'stiffened' anyone), but fired up as I was, I did promise to relate the entire incident to my parents. As I made my way home, this did not seem to be such a good idea, but I was committed to it and could not lose face with my classmates. That night, slowly but surely, I related the whole story and hopefully established my innocence. Surprisingly Dad seemed to take on board what I said and, wonder of wonders, asked, 'What would you like me to do?' This was better than I had hoped for, so I said, 'I would maybe like you to go along to the school and relate what I have told you and ...' I was not sure what I wanted. Dad thought for a while and then said, 'Right I will do that if that's what you want, but can I ask you one question?'

'Of course,' I said. This was wonderful. Dad was taking my side.

'Son,' he said, 'I believe you are innocent in this instance, but can I ask, have there been times in the past where you have not been innocent and maybe deserved to be punished but escaped punishment for whatever reason?'

I had to admit that indeed that was often the case. 'Then,' said Dad, 'maybe it all evens out. The teacher was wrong, but you too have been wrong at times, but I will still go - if you want me to.'

'No Dad,' I said, 'let's leave it there.'

I have often thought of that incident. Not for the last time did I learn something from Dad, who was perhaps one of the most gracious, tolerant and understanding of men, and always saw the best in everyone.

I have so many memories of my mother. She coped with pain uncomplainingly, was devoted to my father and fiercely proud of me. As a child I figured she had the ability to know what I was about to do before I did it. I think all mothers have this ability. She had a thing about water. So did I. I loved guddling in it, and the nearby Kilbarchan Burn offered many opportunities. Maybe it was not so much the water that was her problem but the fact that you might get your feet wet. 'Don't play in the burn' was a mantra in our house.

Of course, I played in the burn. There was never a problem if you did not get your feet wet. I believed I had the grace of a gazelle to skip and jump from stepping-stone to stepping-stone. In truth, I was probably more like an inebriated hippo and inevitably, my shoes would become submerged. I have always considered myself a creative thinker and even then, the first green shoots of creativity were developing. I would remove the offending shoe or shoes, wring out the socks, and then lash them against the nearest wall. The purpose of this was to drive out any moisture. It worked. However, it also had the result that it caused a considerable elongation of the sock. The ankle socks, or knee socks, got so long they could have stretched up beyond the thigh. I say, 'could' because the by-product of 'lengthening' the sock had the effect of reducing the space where you would insert your foot. Indeed, reducing it so much sometimes it was an effort to get any more than your big toe into the aperture. With strenuous effort, it was usually possible to get the foot and leg into the still damp sock. There was always a risk to circulation, but to me it was a worthwhile risk to avoid maternal wrath and the inevitable penalty for 'getting your feet wet'. Nevertheless, Mum still knew. In retrospect, maybe the fact my knee length socks still disappeared up my shorts had something to do with it.

The Mission Hall was big in my life and Sundays involved the morning meeting that usually lasted almost an hour and a half. Looking back, it was a strange sort of service with many people taking part as 'the spirit led them'. I must say, rather irreverently, I wonder if their speaking was more to do with their inability to contain their verbosity rather than any connection with the Holy Spirit. There were often long and painful silences during the service that always culminated in the celebration of the Lord's Supper or Communion or the Eucharist as others would know it. On Sunday afternoons I had Sunday school,

Sunday evenings - the Gospel meeting. My Uncle Bert Miller led the Sunday school.

There is little doubt that if Bert had been around today he would have been arrested. He drove a delivery lorry for West Coast Transport. Every day he would be besieged by children knocking at his door. 'Bertie, where are ye gaun the day. Can we come?' Almost invariably his reply would be, 'Aye, jump in the back.' And so it was half the weans in the village would pile in the back of his lorry. He would deliver a variety of goods all over Renfrewshire and beyond. Incredibly, he never lost one child! Today, Health and Safety and Child Protection would be on his back. But Bertie Miller was a legend. He had a love for children and was perhaps, just a little bit of the child himself.

Back in the fifties, the Sunday school of the Mission Hall would be packed and the trip to such exotic spots as Largs, Troon, Seamill and even Balloch Park were anticipated with great excitement.

Often the Mission Hall would stage what were called 'Tea Meetings' on a Saturday evening. In the mid-fifties, the Brethren were not in favour of TV, even the radio was frowned upon. Sunday papers were also out -- so nae Broons or Oor Willie. Perhaps the tea meetings passed for entertainment. Sometimes there would be singers, testimonies about how people became Christian, and a fire and brimstone talk. All good stuff, but the highlight was the tea.

As I grew older, I was allowed to sit with my friends rather than with my mum and dad. We chose to sit upstairs, a good vantage point to see the Alsop girls who had come up from the Hexham area and were members of the Mission Hall. They were bonnie lassies indeed, Ruth, Naomi and Eunice -- good biblical names.

The sandwiches, cakes and buns were the best part of the evening. When devoured there was also the opportunity to create fright with the paper bag which contained them. When inflated and held tight it could then be smacked between the hands to create a decent bang. Apart from scaring the elderly folk, it had the unfortunate result of attracting attention to ourselves, resulting in our removal from our vantage point.

Another ploy was to drop portions of cake or bun into the organist's teacup, which was usually parked on top of the organ right beneath the gallery. Unfortunately, my Dad was the organist so that ploy usually landed me in trouble with the customary excuse of, 'it wisnae me,' being ignored.

My circle of friends began to grow. By this time, I was meeting other children who attended the Sunday school and, more importantly, whose parents were members of the Mission Hall. Cliff Gibb, Angus Gawn, Ken Munday and my cousin Jack Miller, became my social circle.

One Saturday a friend and I ignored the dilapidated 'Keep Out' and 'Private' signs at the Grove estate. We knew the place well enough so we made our way to a large shed in the grounds. It was suggested it had at one time been an aircraft hangar. It was certainly big enough. We had no plans, just a couple of youngsters at a loose end. It was a cold winter's day so we built a fire. We began to explore the shed, climbing over plasterboard and timber. Meanwhile our fire had taken on a life of its own and showed signs of getting out of hand. We beat it with pieces of plasterboard, indeed anything that was to hand but fire was winning. We looked at each other and in an instant realised the battle was lost and we took off. That day we would have rivalled Usain Bolt as we departed the scene, hurdling a wall and running across a couple of fields so keeping us away from Kilbarchan's streets. We skirted the village using pathways and open fields, eventually reaching a vantage point where we could see the fire blazing away and hear the ringing from fire brigade tenders rushing to the conflagration. Returning home, our respective parents were able to tell us how we had missed all the drama. I suppose it was a lesson how our unintentional, but stupid action, could have put life at risk. What I remember is that for the next month even the very sight of the 'polis' had a devastating effect on my bowels.

My relationship with cousin Jack in those early years was, sadly, to be broken for some years. His father, also Jack, like all of the Miller family, was a hard-working man. He had a full-time job in an engineering works, JD Tappers, but decided to take on the responsibility of running a smallholding in the village of Erskine. They had a few acres and some livestock including a number of hens. Cousins Jack and Jim along with their father had quite a business selling eggs around the area. Jim was called up for National Service in the Royal Navy, but the egg-run continued until Uncle Jack took ill and sadly passed away. The family decided to emigrate to Australia where the older sister Helen resided. I will never forget the night when Aunt Bell, my cousins Jack, Jim and Robert pulled out of St Enoch's station on the London train en route to Australia. The united Miller family, uncles, aunts, cousins waved them good-bye and tried to sing through their tears, 'God be with you till we meet again.' My goodness we were good at emotion. Eventually, Aunt Bell, Jack and Robert were to return to Scotland and my friendship with Jack, who was more like a brother, took up again. Cousin Jim had fallen in love and he and his bride-to-be, Helen, stayed in Australia.

On my 15th birthday, I was given as a present a magnificent 10 speed, iridescent blue, Dawes racing bike. I was off. The world was my oyster and I thought nothing of cycling to Largs and back via Greenock along with Cliff, Gus and Ken. Our favourite was to cycle down through Renfrewshire's leafy lanes and catch the Erskine Ferry (the days before the bridge). Once on the other side we would get behind the slipstream of the Balloch bus. Had it ever stopped unexpectedly, I would not have been here to tell the tale. We would then come through Dumbarton and, taking the back road through Bonhill and Jamestown, reach Balloch and Loch Lomondside. Sometimes we would even cycle up to Luss and on the odd occasion, over to Arrochar, back through Helensburgh and home.

Strangely enough, Bonhill was often in the news. It was around the late fifties and the minister of the parish was hitting the headlines. The Rev Allan G. Hasson had a passion for flute bands and white horses! He was grand master of the Orange Order and was a regular feature in the newspapers, initially for marrying runaway brides who took advantage of Scotland's marriage laws. Many from abroad, mostly

Holland, but also some who had by-passed Gretna and come to Bonhill. Allan and his long-suffering wife, Martha, often put a roof over their heads.

Allan did, of course, ride a white horse through the main street of Alexandria at the head of the orange order march. It is said that youths had painted the white horse with green stripes. This is apocryphal but what is true is that when the hordes marched up the Main Street they passed Gallone's ice cream shop. Many of the marchers had developed both a hunger and thirst. The thirst could be satisfied at the Old Vale Bar and their hunger at Gallone's. Anything edible was voraciously eaten, the shelves were cleared of everything except one lonely jar of 'soor plooms'. Those Orange lads were never happy with the colour green!

Then there was the 'big story'. Allan was accused of embezzling £10,000 from the Orange Order and had left for Canada in the early sixties. When he returned a decade or so later he was immediately arrested at Prestwick Airport. He was charged and tried at the High Court in Glasgow, defended by no less a man than Joe Beltrami (a notable Catholic layman). Apparently, the case made legal history. The judge is said to have misdirected the jury and the case was judged to be 'Not Proven'. Little did I think that many years later I would succeed the Rev Allan. Though many have branded him a bigot, others from all faiths and none, would testify to being helped by the man. I have been left to conclude that this maverick of a man was a latter day Robin Hood who robbed the rich to pay the poor. It is generally held that Allan Hasson did not personally benefit from the so called embezzlement.

Still traveling on my bike, I would cycle down the hill past Ian McColl's garage. Ian was at that time the Scotland football manager. He had played for Rangers and had the good fortune to marry Bonhill lass, Jessie McLean. I was beginning to know Bonhill, but I never expected I would later spend more than half my life there.

CHAPTER TWO

WORK, DECISIONS AND MARRIAGE

SCHOOL was soon over and worked loomed. My first job was as a stores clerk at the Glasgow Corporation Transport's Bus Works office at 147 Butterbiggens Road. I started at the princely sum of £4.7/6 per week. The job was excruciatingly dull and boring. It was my task to monitor the outgoings and incomings of everything from a needle to an anchor. I had to keep a tally of nuts, bolts, fibreglass wings and panels for the buses and even the quaintly named modesty panels. Yes, eventually I did have to ask... Apparently, it was some sort of guard that wound up the stairs of buses and trams and prevented the potential pervert from looking up the skirts of women who decided to go upstairs for a fly puff. So now, you know!

I was desperate to drive. Dad was the proud possessor of an Armstrong Siddeley car, which was classy for those days, but he trusted me, and with the additional help of the local driving instructor Johnny Borland, I passed first time. Even better, Dad let me drive on my own, not bad at age 17 being entrusted with a limo.

My boss was Jimmy Campbell. He did not rate me. After a couple of years working there, I was slightly surprised when I received a letter from the Personnel Department advising me that I had been promoted and that my weekly salary was almost doubled. Oh joy, oh rapture! Being a well brought up lad, I duly went to thank my boss, believing him to be instrumental in my elevation. He tersely denied all knowledge and offered the opinion that if it had been anything to do with him he would not have employed me to clean the toilets. I came down to earth with a bump.

I got the message, and fairly soon afterwards left the Bus Works office. After dabbling briefly in sales, I landed a job in a travel agency in Causeyside Street, Paisley with OSA Tours. My boss was a man called Dan Hawthorn. He believed I could walk on water. I could sell holidays! If you came in to book for Rothesay, I sold you Majorca. I am actually not a salesman. I can only sell something to someone who wants to buy in the first place. Does that make sense? Everyone who enters a travel agency wants to go a holiday so if you could not get Lloret De Mar at the Glasgow Fair I made sure I booked you somewhere that was warm and in close proximity to bars and entertainment.

Dan thought I was a genius. His politics were certainly to the left and he put that into practice by instituting a scheme that ensured if the company did well, we did well. He paid commission. I would have died for Dan Hawthorn. I would not have crossed the road for Jimmy Campbell, but I am hugely indebted to those two guys. They taught me a lesson, which has been fundamental to everything I have sought to do in life. You achieve nothing by pulling people down but you achieve everything by affirming them, encouraging them and trusting them. I deplore those who take away people's self-esteem and self-belief. It is no way to manage people and it is very counterproductive.

I have met many bullies in my time. Some were intimidating thugs who roamed the streets, but I also found them in industry, business, and schools, in the Health Service and even in the Church. I deplored it. I firmly believe that you can get the most out of people when you support them.

While working for Glasgow Corporation Transport I lived through what was for me, one of the most terrifying episodes in my life - The Cuban Crisis. For 13 days, three men, Nikita Khrushchev, Jack Kennedy and Fidel Castro gambled with the fate of the planet and I followed the news with obsessive interest. The world teetered on the brink of a nuclear holocaust. I would travel to my work often thinking I might not make it home. Recent television documentaries and articles have made me realise how near we came to lighting the blue touch paper, which would have ushered in the Third World War. Unlike WW1 and the folly of trench warfare or even the horrors of WW2, with its concentration camps and holocaust, the bombing of Coventry and Dresden, WW3 would be, by contrast, a quick affair and the lucky ones would be those who perished initially in the fireball.

Later evidence has confirmed that I had good reason to be worried. JFK opposed the hawks in his government who wished to take action against the Russians. Curtis Le May was a hero of the U.S. Air Force. He has been described as a 'remarkably creative tactician'. From early on he argued that, 'if you are going to use military force, then you ought to use overwhelming military force.' His men called him 'Iron Ass'. I would have omitted the word 'iron'. He was for war. He stated he wanted to, 'Fry Cuba.' The military in the USA were for striking decisively. The American air force was circling the Soviet borders like wolves waiting for the kill. Kennedy stood alone. Nikita Khrushchev was also under threat from many in the politburo who advised him he must be decisive. They feared the Albanians and Chinese would misinterpret any show of weakness. Later he confessed that it would be no consolation for him to know, as he sat amidst the smouldering ruins of his beloved country, that he had been strong and the outcome was the destruction of his country and that of America. Thank God John Fitzgerald Kennedy acted with restraint and thank God (the God Nikita did not believe in) the Russian leader showed similar restraint.

The Cuban crisis hastened a decision I had been postponing for some time. Entry into full fellowship of the Mission Hall was via baptism, none of your sprinkling stuff - full immersion - a right 'dookin'. Most brethren assemblies had a 'tank' built underneath the platform. Scare stories circulated that you were expected to be naked under the white robe they provided. Rumour also had it when you entered the water the robe would ride up and be a threat to your modesty. That was a worry, mind you that was dwarfed by the thought of meeting St Peter at the pearly gates perched on top of a mushroom shaped cloud and having to explain why I hadn't been baptised. So, Nikita, Jack and Fidel gave me the push I needed, I was baptised.

I am thankful for my Mission Hall background. There were so many pluses, but one or two negatives. In retrospect there seemed to be a concentration on what we should not be doing - no smoking, no drinking, no dancing, no pictures and, for girls, no make-up. All this, rather than a concentration on what we should be doing. There was also the threat of Hell Fire. At the age of seven I was led to believe I was destined for HELL. Furthermore, the preacher would often tell us that if Jesus came for the saved, the unsaved would be left behind. As a little boy, I remember waking up in the middle of the night and going through to my parents' bedroom just to check that Jesus had not taken them and left me. I kept wondering if I was 'saved'. I had asked Jesus to come into my heart, but what if it had not worked? What if he hadn't heard me? Was I sincere enough? Such faith wrestling at such a tender age! In retrospect, I now firmly believe this approach would have found no approval from the man of Nazareth who had such time for children. Terrifying children into belief surely must be wrong.

Something else was happening in my life about this time. Though still greatly involved in the Mission Hall, I had also become involved in the local Church of Scotland Youth Fellowship. By this time, I was in my late teens. On a Sunday night, I would attend the Gospel Hall, then slip out during the last hymn, and head over to Kilbarchan West Church hall where I took part in debates, listened to speakers and of course met girls. The Youth Fellowship became a great marriage bureau. Much as I owe the Mission Hall for my Christian upbringing, it was narrow and restrictive. The break with the Mission Hall came suddenly and unexpectedly. Indeed, it is distinctly possible that, but for the challenge presented to me by one of the 'Elders' then, I might still have been there. Unexpectedly he cornered me and asked me if I was with them or with the Church. The answer was simple; I was with the Mission Hall. He then told me I was to cease my involvement with the Church. It was 'them' or 'us', he told me, and with the impulsivity of youth I said 'then you leave me no choice. I see no conflict in my present loyalties, but if you force me to choose, which I think is wrong, then, you leave me no option.'

With tears in my eyes, I left the Mission Hall that night. I dreaded telling my parents. I spent a miserable night at the Youth Fellowship and returned home. I confessed what I had done and feared their disapproval. I was wrong. They were both understanding and supportive. How could I have doubted them?

My father continued to worship at the Mission Hall, playing the organ Sunday by Sunday but I do not believe my mother ever returned, which saddened me. That night lives with me. It was a hurtful moment but in retrospect, it was for the best. It was also a lesson I learned and I made a decision that I would never force any young person to make that sort of choice -- and I do not think I ever have. I also found it interesting that no one ever asked why I disappeared from the Mission Hall. Who knows? Maybe they were glad!

So the following Sunday I sat in the West Kirk Pews. Suddenly I was aware there was a big new world out there that was prepared to challenge my views and thinking. I soon was sucked into this and for the next six or seven years it became a huge part of my life. Initially my views on Christianity were pretty set and it is to the great credit of Rev Andrew Kerr, Minister at Kilbarchan West Kirk, that he did not chuck this young upstart out on his ear. Andrew Kerr had a wonderfully long ministry in Kilbarchan and during his tenure; three lads went forward to the Christian ministry, Eoin Shedden, Bill McKaig and myself. That says something about his influence. However, initially it was a culture shock. Instead of singing the upbeat hymns of the Mission Hall, I was singing hymns, which initially appeared, to me to be 'awfy dreich', sung with a lack of enthusiasm and often at a funereal pace. Despite this, I settled into my new spiritual home.

The Youth Fellowship became my complete passion. It was not unusual for over 100 of Kilbarchan's young folk to pack into the church hall on Sunday night. We debated the big issues of life and promised each other we would change the world. Some of the friendships forged in those days still remain. We staged three huge charity concerts in the Kelburn Cinema in Paisley and filled the place (1700 plus people) and charged five shillings a ticket.

We arranged some great social nights in the church hall and the Kirk Session trusted us. The favourites were the Barn Dances, straw bales placed around the walls acting as seating and also a soft landing place for the girls, who during the execution of a Strip the Willow were often spun off the arms of the over enthusiastic lads by centrifugal force. The churchyard outside the halls also provided an appropriate place for romantic assignations. Not all assignations took place there however. Cousin Jack was in the privileged position of having 'wheels'. It was an old van but still WHEELS. His mother had asked him to get rid of a mattress, which was surplus to the family's requirements. It was loaded into the back of the van, but instead of it being dumped, it remained there. His mother was becoming increasingly impatient with its presence and one night, in no uncertain terms, it was made clear it had to go. Where could we dump it? Fly tipping was as yet an unheard of crime. Recycling was still light-years away, so where? Driving along a quiet road on the outskirts of Kilbarchan, he stopped. Instantly I knew his intention. The road skirted the perimeter wall of one of Kilbarchan's grander mansions. This was to be its destiny. We hauled it out and, with manic tears running down our cheeks, we heaved it onto the top of the wall where it became snagged on little iron spikes positioned to deter would be housebreakers and perhaps disposers of redundant mattresses. A final heave and it was over the wall. There was a huge splash on the other side. We grasped the iron spikes and hauled ourselves upwards to observe the scene and there bobbing away gently on the private lake, shafts of moonlight dancing on the ripples, was Jake's mattress. It was in some ways quite picturesque.

A group of us from the YOUTH FELLOWSHIP took off on a grand adventure to travel Europe in a minibus. Cousin Jack Miller being the senior member of the party at around 24, Elspeth Raeburn at 23, myself at 22, then Helen Reid and Jane Trushell probably around 18 or 19 at the time, and Eric Finney, Malcolm Reid, Billy McKaig, Gordon Sharp and Willie Atherton, probably all around 17 or 18.

Eric's dad, Fred, worked with McIntyre Greenock, the Vauxhall dealer, and he helped us acquire a Bedford Dormobile minibus for the princely sum of £100. In that vehicle, we journeyed from Kilbarchan down to Dover, across on the ferry to Ostend, then down through Belgium stopping at Bruges before travelling onward to Germany. Once there we continued, via the Autobahn, to the walled city of Rothenberg. Some of us climbed up the rickety wooden stairs of one of those typical Bavarian churches with the 'upturned onion' dome on the top. We emerged into daylight on the smallest little landing imaginable and a safety rail that did not reach my knees. That was the only barrier between me and a precipitous drop onto the market below. I froze, then grabbed that dome and hung on like grim death. Behind me, also wishing to see 'the view', were my cousin Jack, Willie Atherton and Gordon Sharp. Seeing the terror on my face, they urged me to make my way gingerly back down stairs. I was having none of it. I was staying there forever if need be. A lifelong friendship with these guys was forged that day. They loosened my grip and passed me from hand to hand until I reached the safety of the stairs. I do not think I had a fear of heights before that but since then standing on the top of the kitchen table gives me goose bumps.

The journey continued through Southern Germany visiting the castle of Neuschwanstein, which featured in the film Chitty Chitty Bang Bang. It was built by 'Mad' King Ludwig ll of Bavaria. He built a series of grand edifices often adorning them with Wagnerian scenes. That day its visual impact was almost ethereal. Bands of low-lying mist obscured the lower structure and the pinnacles appeared to emerge from the clouds into an azure sky. No wonder Walt Disney claimed it was the inspiration for the fairy tale castle in Sleeping Beauty. We travelled onto to Salzburg where we stayed for a week. What a wonderful city. It is

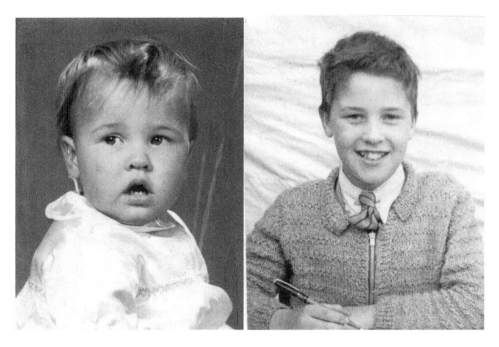

Even at an early age, the mouth is open.

First year Johnstone High.

The Armstrong Siddeley car in which Ian passed his test, but not at that age.

Kilbarchan Youth Fellowship trip to Europe. Eight countries in 1967.

Our wedding, 1st of August, 1969, with our parents

like Edinburgh with the castle dominating the skyline. I had been there before while staying at a Christian Youth Centre in Upper Austria. I just fell in love with it, its music, the zithers, quaint streets, fabulous cakes and of course the connection with the Sound of Music and all those iconic scenes. Indeed, one night a few of us were set to have a dip in the Salzburg fountains when a passer-by warned us the polizie took a very dim view of that and a compulsory overnight stay in the local cop shop would be a strong possibility. A debate ensued. Some were for chancing it, probably influenced by the girls, who urged restraint. I'm glad to say that sanity prevailed.

We then travelled back through Innsbruck and into Liechtenstein and then onto Switzerland, staying at Interlaken for a week, going up the Jungfrau, throwing snowballs at each other in July. We travelled through France, where Willie encountered the wonders of the French loos. In desperation and with a pained expression he informed us there were no toilets on the camp site only some sort of shower arrangement with a big hole in the floor.

Then it was the Channel and the long haul home. A journey of over 3000 miles undertaken in just over three weeks, visiting eight countries. The journey was not without mishap. While travelling over the Susten Pass and dropping down to Meiringen in Switzerland, cousin Jack seemed to have a worried look. He was continually pumping the brake pedal. 'There is something up with the brakes,' he said. Lack of stopping ability was going to be a problem as we negotiated the hairpin bends down the mountainside but either by good driving with Jake at the wheel, or me praying, we made it and continued on our journey.

The brakes eventually did give up in Birmingham. Thankfully and fortuitously, Jake had an uncle who lived close-by. He was a motor mechanic and, bless his heart, Uncle Will got us on the road again. Mind you, we had to stay overnight. Not to be deterred, we just pitched our tents under the cover of darkness on a green patch in the middle of a housing estate. I think the residents thought the tinkers had arrived ... Little did they know how near the truth they were.

On return, we allowed some friends of ours to use the van. They were known as the Concords, one of Scotland's first gospel bands. They were stuck for transport and so borrowed our bus and, unfortunately, wrote it off. However, we got £150 back from the insurance company. Not at all bad. A three-week holiday and £50 in profit. Five of the group still keep in pretty close contact. Jack and Helen married not long after their return.

The following year I visited a great aunt in America. She had left these shores many years before from Greenock. She was to marry Bill McColl whose roots were also in Scotland and they were to prove the most wonderful hosts ensuring there would be nothing in the great city of Washington I did not see. America was a wonderful experience. Being a travel agent, I was able to fly out on a discounted ticket (costing £19) with BOAC to Washington DC and returning from Montreal to Greenock on the Empress of Canada in a single cabin for the grand total of £22.

I travelled from Washington to Canada on a Greyhound bus up through Maryland, Pennsylvania and New York State. For part of the journey, I sat with a young Amish man who was a protester against the war in Vietnam. He told me of his unusual life style. No electricity, none of the things we take for granted and travelling into town with a horse and buggy. Mind you, I should have asked him what he was doing on a bus.

En-route to Toronto, I departed my transportation to visit the Niagara Falls. It was very early in the morning, around 5 or 6am. Dawn was breaking. There were few people about. I was dressed in a kilt, carrying a large suitcase and the bus terminal at Niagara was some distance from the falls. Lugging the suitcase was tiring so I decided to park it in large clump of bushes while I went on to see the sights. Few things in life have had such an impact on me. The raging turbulent torrent of water that dashed headlong over the falls was mesmeric. I was silent and in awe of this incredible work of nature. Silence does not come easily to me and soon I wanted to share my thoughts with someone. However, there was no one there. It was so early in the morning. Then I heard footsteps. I was about to share with this complete stranger my awe-struck feelings when he spoke in a broad Glasgow accent. 'Is that it then?' Actually, it sounded more phonetically like, 'izzatiten?' I did not respond but just walked away silently.

On returning to collect my suitcase from the shrubbery there were two women nearby engaged in conversation. I hung around hoping their dialogue would soon end. It did not. Impatiently I marched into the shrubs, kilt flying, and emerged with my suitcase. They looked astonished and doubtless, it added fuel to their belief that the Scots are a bit tight. They would probably say later that day 'my goodness we saw one fellow, obviously from Scotland, who would not even pay to check in his luggage when visiting the Falls. How mean is that?'

Something also happened during my stay in Washington, which was to cause me to ponder the possibility of a life changing decision. My aunt and uncle attended New York Avenue Church, a famous church with a rich history. Abe Lincoln worshipped there. More recently, the minister was Peter Marshall. Peter was a Coatbridge lad who became chaplain to the US Senate. He sadly died young but his legacy remained. They even made a film about his life called 'A man called Peter', starring Richard Todd. In the late sixties, the minister at New York Avenue was George Docherty, also a Scot, and in my brief time there, George took an interest in me and wrote to the Divinity Faculty in Glasgow suggesting I would be an able candidate.

In fairness, George Docherty had not jumped the gun because there had been a developing feeling within that I should become a minister. I was fighting against it but it would not go away. In one way, it was quite easy to fight against it because I figured ministers had to go to university and to get to university you needed to pass exams. I left school having graduated with honours at playing the fool, so O levels, Highers and University degrees where dreams, but still this feeling would not go away.

I loved my job as a travel agent and had been promoted at age 21 by my mentor Dan Hawthorn to be manager of a small agency in Johnstone. Life was good. Why would I spoil it by going back to 'school'? However, George Docherty, Dr Arthur Fawcett, my former school chaplain, and Andrew Kerr, my own minister, began to convince me it was something I should consider.

Eventually I made a decision. If the Almighty were indeed giving me a push towards the ministry, I would prove to Him how this just could not be. I would attempt to jump those hurdles on the long road to being accepted as a candidate, fully expecting to fail. I started night school and did tolerably well. I then persuaded Dan Hawthorn to let me attend Langside College part-time and, amazingly, the qualifications began to pile up. Enough to gain me access to Glasgow University. However, the church, surely the church, would find me out. I would have to present myself as a candidate for the ministry and go to selection school. That would be the hurdle to trip me. I went, I passed and I was accepted. Now I was beginning to run out of excuses. Still, I had my doubts.

I am almost ashamed to admit how the final push came. One of our Youth Fellowship took ill and landed in the Royal Infirmary in Glasgow. Anne would have been about 17 and still attending John Neilson High School in Paisley. While leaving hospital one night with her parents, I realised they were quite visibly upset. It appeared Anne's life was at risk. That night I did something, which I would never encourage anyone to do, and yet I know many have done it. I bargained with God. 'Get the lass well,' I prayed. That would be the final sign. She got well and for me there was no going back. Anne was told she might not have children. She has four. She and husband Gordon (one of the minibus trip), are among our dearest friends to this day.

The Concords and their music had also become a great part in my life. Gordon Webster, Ian Ramsden, Lesley Mitchell and Dougie Watt. They were such talented musicians and they performed most Saturday nights. They invited me to come along and speak, often at church cafes, church youth groups, or mission hall events. They performed at the

Usher Hall, they made records, and at the time of The Troubles, we went to Ireland and performed at the Belfast City Halls. It was a great time and I am glad to say that Gordon, Ian and myself, remain friends.

On return from America, I continued my activity with the Youth Fellowship. One Sunday night our group decided to attend a special screening of 'The War Game' in Sherwood Church, Paisley. The film made by Peter Watkins, depicting the horrors of nuclear war. It was considered too horrific for television or mainstream cinema and was accordingly granted a special licence to be shown privately to groups and clubs. It was suggested that nursing staff should be on hand to attend to anyone who experienced distress during the viewing. By this time, I was ardently anti-nuclear and did not need persuasion to attend. A brief conversation took place between a Miss Joan Parr and me as we alighted from the bus on Glasgow Road, Paisley. Although I did not realise it myself, this was to be one of those seminal moments in my life. Realising she was new, I just said to her, 'Hello I am Ian Miller.' She simply said, 'I know.' Actually, I knew fine who she was. Often when dashing home from Paisley on a Western SMT bus to Kilbarchan for a quick lunch, Joan would be on the upper deck. Even then, she struck me as a bonnie lass. She would be about 15 at the time and I a mature 21. Too young for me! She always looked cool and very chic in a tight short skirt and if she did give me a second glance, which I doubt, it would simply be to say to herself, Too old for me. However, as we alight from that bus she is now 17 and I am 23. The gap is still the same but does not seem so much anymore. I do not say that her attraction to me was immediate.

Joan had a few young men in tow, but I was determined. Around that time an elderly minister, the Rev William Burnside, had come in to book a holiday to Oberammergau. He had lost his wife some years before. Some months later, he returned looking rather shamefaced. He asked me to change the booking from a single room to a double room. I asked him who was going with him. He answered that it was 'a young lady'. I think she was about 60 at the time. He said to me, 'I have pursued her for many months and eventually she capitulated.' Well, eventually Joan 'capitulated' and we became an item.

After a relatively short period, I began to think this was the ONE, and it appeared she thought likewise. We agreed we should get engaged. This was probably not much more than a year after we started 'going out'. We decided we would become engaged at Christmas 1968. By this time, she is 18 and I am 24 and about to give up my job and undertake a university course lasting five years. Any self-respecting father would wish to ensure his daughter's financial security. Could we afford to be married? Why the rush? Well in some ways, the rush was financial. If we got married before I started the university, I qualified for a married student's allowance. If we had any children before the end of the course, then I qualified for another pay out. So let's get married before the course starts. Problem was, how could I persuade Joan's father that there was any degree of logic in our plans? I asked Joan to brief him. She kept putting it off. I would ask, 'Have you spoken to your mum and dad yet?' The answer was invariably, 'I will do it tomorrow, next week, whenever.' Time was rushing towards Christmas. Eventually, she said she had spoken to her parents and I was to come up to the family home at 71 Wheatlands Drive and speak to Willie and Lizzie Parr.

I came prepared with a financial breakdown of my income for the next few years. What I would get with the enhanced student grant, which was a considerable sum in today's terms, plus Joan's wages. This would be in addition to what I would hope to earn as a postman during the Christmas Holidays, and from work at the Locherfield Tannery during the summer holidays. It was all there. Joan took her mother into the kitchen and I started my sales pitch. Willie listened in silence. I became less and less confident for he was not responding. I closed my case with those words, 'so you don't need to worry. I will be able to support your daughter. What do you think? '

I refrained from saying, 'for goodness sake speak to me.' Well he did, he just said in his own inimitable way, 'a huvnae a clue whit ye are talking aboot.'

To this day, I do not know whether Joan did prime him, though she says she did, or whether he was just having me on. The latter is more likely. In any case, I was accepted. Joan and I were engaged on the 24th December 1968. I put the ring on her finger during the midnight service and Joan proudly showed it off outside after the service. Boy was I a happy man! It was agreed that we would indeed be married before the university term started and the date of 1st August 1969 was chosen. Joan and her mother went into hyper-drive, researching places for the reception. The Rev Andrew Kerr agreed to marry us, coming back from holiday just the day before. Eventually it was decided the reception would be in The Silver Thread, a hotel in Paisley. Photographers and bands were duly arranged. My great-aunt and great-uncle from Washington DC would fly in to join us. Aunt Nellie had not been in Scotland since leaving as an 18-year-old.

It was a great day. Joan looked like a princess. Willie Parr scrubbed up well and my best man Willie Atherton and I looked about as unimportant as groom and best man should. After all, the wedding is all about the bride.

We honeymooned in Torquay, which was always a bone of contention for Joan. I was still at that time a travel agent and could have had access to cheap holidays abroad.

Then it was back to our first house, 21 High Barholm in Kilbarchan. A two bed roomed flat with high ceilings, wonderful ornamental cornicing and a loo on the 'stair heid landing.' Fairly soon with the help of a local authority grant and the skill of our dear building friend Eddie McMurray a new pink bathroom suite was installed with a corner bath. This was sybaritic luxury. Eddie and Dorothy McMurray were such good friends, we had done most of our courting - or 'winching' as it was known locally - while 'baby-sitting' their two sons, Harry and Eric. This flat become a magnet for many of our unmarried friends, often landing at our house to watch the Friday night horror movie on STV. Every Thursday night there was often a card school. No money but a lot of fun. I was still involved in the church and running a bible class. Many of those youngsters in their mid-teens also spent time at our house, often staying the night.

In June of every year, the village of Kilbarchan comes alive for Lilias Day, the origins of which are lost in history. The houses are decorated, floral arches are erected and a parade of people dressed as historical characters from Kilbarchan's past walk through the streets. For many years, this tradition died, but then in the late sixties Ann Grieve and Helen Fulton revived it. Indeed, many of those born in the village were less than enthusiastic but Helen and Ann pursued their dream and on the first Saturday in June of the year 1968, it happened.

The Kilbarchan Pipe Band led the procession through the village streets. Behind them would be St Barchan and his monks stopping briefly at the steeple square at which point St Barchan would leave the procession, knock loudly on the steeple door and invite Habbie Simpson, whose effigy sits in a niche just below the steeple clock, to join the procession. Habbie was a well-known piper in the village in the 1500s, and people born and living in the village are known as 'Habbies'.

For many years, I was privileged to play the part of St Barchan.

Behind all this were over 20 imaginatively decorated trucks entered by the village's many organisations. Eventually the parade wound its way through the village ending at the public park and then all the fun of Kilbarchan's Gala day commenced and this tradition continues to this very day. Joan and I were privileged to be part of this for quite a few years.

I also remember the day the Queen came to visit the village. A wee lad in the crowd, unable to see, climbed a lamppost like a latter-day Zacchaeus, the tax collector who climbed a tree to see Jesus. He suffered abuse from those around, threatening to tell his Mammy and warning him of dire consequences. I wondered if Zacchaeus suffered the same abuse. If he did, I hope he dealt with it with the same disdain as the wee lad. He was unmoved by the threats of parental retribution and had a grandstand view of Her Majesty's limousine as it progressed up the Steeple Brae. It stopped at the foot of the steps and she exited.

Crowds mobbed around. She then climbed the steps where a few of us stood dressed in our Lilias Day outfits. The Queen stopped and asked me who I was meant to be and I told her. Apparently a voice in the crowd was heard to say, 'she is talking to Ian Miller; she will be there a' day.' I was to meet Her Majesty again later. I often wondered if she remembered me. If she did, she never mentioned it!

CHAPTER THREE

UNIVERSITY

- AND THEN WHERE WOULD I GO?

THE month of October had me standing in the cloisters of Glasgow University waiting to matriculate. This was new to me. I think it just meant to enrol but sounded like a surgical procedure. I entered academia with fear and trepidation. I had left school and excelled at nothing apart from being a nuisance. The cloisters of Glasgow University were intimidating and I felt like a gatecrasher at a party.

The first year of divinity for mature students involved one year of arts, generally studying English Literature, Moral Philosophy, European History and New Testament Greek.

My fellow students were interesting. Some were very intense and into deep and meaningful theological debate. I think clerics of a by-gone age would debate about how many angels could stand on the head of a pin. We had folk like that, often engaging the professors and lecturers in heated dialogue. There were also those who knew that it was 'heads down for a few years' which would enable them to do what they felt was their calling. I probably leant towards that group. There were also those who were quick to escape from lectures to find 'spiritual comfort' in some hostelry or other. I had some degree of affinity with them as well.

Sadly, I have not kept up with very many of fellow students, most of whom were destined for the parish ministry. However, I quickly formed a strong bond of friendship with John Beck and Duncan Hunter. Bill Hewitt also became one of our number (Bill later became a Moderator of the General Assembly). He was not that fond of attending classes, but when he was there, he enjoyed our company and we enjoyed his.

John Beck was a character with an irreverent sense of humour. The divinity faculty met in the old Trinity College a famous Glasgow landmark with its twin towers. We also met at South Park Terrace, just across from the main university gates. The sixth form girls from Hillhead Academy used to strut their stuff past our windows. On one occasion, during a dreary lesson on Systematic Theology, John reached over to me and said, 'Ian, when I get out of here I am going to start up a mission for nubile young schoolgirls.' Sadly, I do not think it ever became a reality but it certainly had possibilities.

Duncan was a Lutheran from Springfield, Massachusetts, though you would never have known. He was as Scottish as anyone else in the class was. He had left Caldercruix with his family en route to America. When they arrived, the family was met with the news that his father had died. His father had gone out first to set up home for the rest of the family. Faced with this tragedy they returned home but later were to make their way back to USA to follow their dream. Duncan served in the US military during the Vietnam War and the government recognised his contribution and provided funding for his theology course. During this time, he stayed with an aunt in Caldercruix, his old home. These two fellows have become lifelong friends and though they are now both retired I still see them. They were to be my sanity from 1969-1974.

While on honeymoon, I bought for myself a wonderfully bright, almost lurid pair of red corduroy trousers. Boy was I a dandy! I was so proud of them and wore them to university. After our first set of exams my friend Duncan had a consultation with the Professor of New Testament, the world renowned William Barclay. Willie was a national figure at that time, appearing regularly on Sunday night television. Duncan, exited from his meeting with Willie, said to me, 'either you have done awfy weel or awfy badly, for Willie was asking who you were.'

Duncan tried to give some sort of description, but it did not help. Eventually in desperation, Duncan indicated I had a great fondness for a pair of red trousers. Willie's face lit up, 'The one that wears the cardinal's breeks,' he exclaimed. And that was me. My red trousers served me well, made me recognisable and gave some sort of indication of my political leanings.

Willie Barclay was a wonderful lecturer and I feel privileged to have sat at his feet. As I read his books to this day, I can still hear his gruff compelling voice. His ability to set the New Testament in context was the best. He made the Bible live.

Another character at Trinity College was Professor Murdo Ewan Macdonald, a Harris man whose ability as a storyteller was legendary. He had been a prisoner of war and spent time in Stalag Luft 3, which was immortalised in the film, 'The Great Escape'. Murdo was part of it. Indeed, he did escape but was recaptured. He was also involved in spreading the excavated sand and earth from the tunnels- a little bit here, a little bit there. He had a wonderful, lilting Harris accent and was one the most compelling preachers of his day. He was an avid Celtic supporter, unusual in the Church of Scotland. It was an allegiance that found favour in my eyes. I was delighted when he accepted a subsequent invitation to preach at Bonhill. He told the congregation that I was a 'brilliant student', as I knew he would. He said that about all of his students, but I did not tell the congregation that and just basked in the glory.

Holidays were interesting. At Christmas, I was a postman. I loved it. My first year found me delivering to houses in Kilbarchan. There was one house where a large Alsatian dog seemed to lie in wait for me. As I passed in front of the living room, making my way to the front door, the animal would throw itself at the window barking furiously. It used to scare the wits out me so I decided to sort it out. As it lunged, I swung the postbag in the direction of the window, keeping a tight hold of the bag but hoping to scare the dog. It went berserk, yelping, barking, snarling and threw itself bodily at the window again and the window shattered. I do not know who got the biggest surprise. I did not wait to see but took off at a pace that would have won me an Olympic medal. The following day the window was boarded up and the house was silent. Often I wondered what became of the dog, but I was not for enquiring.

Summer holidays were an education. I learned things that would serve me well in my future vocation. Even then, summer jobs were not always easy to get but I was lucky. Some good Kilbarchan connections helped me land a 16-week stint at the National Chrome Tanning works at Locherfield in Bridge of Weir. What a job! The tanning process involves heat, water and eye watering, lung choking chemicals, the end result of which is surely one the most noxious smells known to man. It lingered, and in the words of Macbeth not 'all the perfumes of Arabia' could sweeten it. After a day at the tannery, I used to leave my working clothes outside the door and dive into a bath.

My job was to brush the suede leather. It was a dusty process and after a few hours, my throat just closed up. I presume the advent of health and safety inspections must have ensured a safer, more congenial working environment for the leather industry. From then on, I used a mask. The company provided none and I often wondered what long-term damage must have been done to the lungs of those who worked there. They were great people, salt of the earth. Mind you if I had been there for longer, I think I would have been agitating for better conditions.

I also worked at times in the drying room, perhaps it might have been better described as the frying room. Working there was like being in an equatorial rain forest, carrying bundles of sodden wet, slippery leather and throwing them over red-hot revolving steel poles. People pay to go and sit in a sauna. I was paid to work in one. Certainly, my summer job, plus the very generous government grant given to a mature student, meant we were not in penury. We had our own flat and no mortgage; we had a colour TV, and even went to Austria for our holidays. Life was good.

As the end of the university course loomed, Joan and I decided to start a family. After a night out with friends, Joan was foully sick. A sickness that went on and on and was confirmed as hyperemesis gravidarum. Joan was pregnant. Sadly, she spent six months of her pregnancy in Ward 32 of the RAH Maternity Unit in Paisley, initially with the sickness and then later with high blood pressure. In due course, Derek Ian Miller entered this world on Christmas Eve 1973. At that time, I was acting as student assistant at Newlands South Church in Glasgow. The minister there was the Rev Alywn McFarlane, a delightful man. On hearing of the names, we had decided on, he said, 'I am sure that he will not be DIM.' I did not know what he was talking about so he explained that is the initials of his name DIM. Derek Ian Miller. So David was inserted. Derek Ian David Miller (DIDM or maybe DIDUM!).

What happiness! After a few days, we brought him home to 21 High Barholm, Kilbarchan. Everyone tells you that a baby changes your life. I don't think anyone realises how much. Derek made a point in the first few months of turning day into night, yelling and wailing. Mind you, he enjoyed music and was particularly fond of Simon and Garfunkel. It was the only thing that seemed to soothe him. I was still at university and studying with a baby around is not easy. I still have a photograph of both of us lying side by side, me reading the New Testament in Greek and Derek looking on as if interested.

The University of Glasgow had a system whereby if you scored over 70 per cent in class exams in a particular subject you did not have to sit the end of term degree exam. Class exams happened at the end of each term and there were three terms. In my first year, I managed to achieve three out of five exemptions. That pattern continued through my years at Glasgow. It made for a worry free and relaxed last term. I was working the system fairly well and if I had exemptions, I started to miss the class lectures on those exempted subjects. On my last year, a classmate informed me that there had been a change. Yes, you got exemption but had to sit the degree exam. You would pass but you had to sit that exam.

This news was a huge shock because I must have missed the entire last term's lectures. With a child keeping us up at night, a few more hours of extra shuteye was desirable. When Derek slept, we slept; but now this shock. I knew my degree was safe but I did not intend to embarrass myself sitting an exam where my knowledge would be zilch, having been in my bed when I should have been in the lecture hall. How could I get out of it? The only way seemed to be to get a medical certificate. Could I make up a story? Would my GP play ball? I thought not. Salvation, however, was offered. A fellow student told me his flatmate's uncle was a GP. He would see me all right and give me a medical certificate. What a relief!

He was as good as his word. I grabbed the certificate with the exam now just days away. I was safe. Later on that night, I thought I had better check as to the precise illness that had caused me to be indisposed in case I had to answer questions. My heart sank. The cause of my absence, according to this piece of paper was, 'venereal disease'. I have a fairly well developed sense of humour but at that moment, it deserted me. Was there a backup plan? I hotfooted it to Gilmorehill the following day to be met by three fellow students grinning from ear to ear. It had all been a wind up.

Late in 1973, we decided to move to a larger house in Johnstone, which was rather bizarrely named Lindertis. It was a rather nice three-bedroomed red sandstone terraced house in leafy Thompson Avenue. University was ending but we had an enjoyable couple of years in Johnstone. June 1974 had me graduating as a Bachelor of Divinity and ready to take the final steps to becoming a minister.

The last hurrah would be the final year dinner, an opportunity to be daft for the last time before we wore our shirts the wrong way round and became respectable. Mind, some of my colleagues had decided to be dull and respectable from Day 1. I was still ready to kick over the traces. The venue was booked - The Bellahouston Hotel in Glasgow, and the speakers arranged, for you can never have any event involving the church without speakers.

It was left to me to arrange the final year handbook, which involved having some pithy saying against each of our classmates' names. Mine simply said, 'He travels in ladies' under wear.' That indeed was true, but I have since grown out of it! I had better explain... During my entire university career, Friday was a quiet day and lectures usually were over by lunchtime. My cousin Jake by this time ran a clothing store. He employed me to deliver women's tights and 'other things' all over the West of Scotland.

Our final year coincided with the divinity faculty's departure from Trinity College to its present base at South Park Terrace. Trinity was, and indeed still is, a majestic part of the Glasgow skyline. Now it provides exclusive residences and no longer will prayers be heard in its hallowed halls unless some poor soul is looking for help with the mortgage. The closure of Trinity, however, provided us with a much longed for opportunity to kidnap the 'alligator'. Why was there an alligator in the divinity faculty? I do not know. Theories abounded to explain its presence. Was it there to provide evidence of 'intelligent design' to aspiring young preachers of a by-gone age? Had it devoured some earnest missionary and for its sins been captured and stuffed?

Whatever the reason it had listened, stony faced and slitty-yellow eyed, to lectures on the Pentateuch and on Moses and his 40-year detour in the desert. We decided to hijack it on the day of dinner. John Beck, who is now retired and living in Stirling, masterminded the exercise. Duncan Hunter (who is in Springfield, Massachusetts, and out of the reach of any repercussion, ecclesiastical or otherwise) was the lookout. I acted as 'the heavy' and getaway driver.

The college was eerily quiet. As we entered the vaulted vestibule, the door creaked. Entrance gained, we glanced right and left listening to hear the sound of Mr Collins' feet (the janny), as we tiptoed down the stair to the 'dunny'.

43

Scattering some curious mice, we began searching for the 'alligator'. We grabbed it quickly, hoisted it onto our shoulders, and began the climb up the stairs hopeful of emerging back into Lyndoch Crescent undetected. We succeeded! Using borrowed ropes, we lashed it to the top of my Hillman Minx and drove through the streets of Glasgow. It made its first and last final year dinner dressed in Professor Willie Barclay's old preaching gown, well aware any attempt to snatch a bite of the leg of a passing waitress would mean its immediate expulsion. It did indeed 'make it through the night' and then was loaded back on top of the Minx and it processed regally along Paisley Road West, through Paisley itself and home to Johnstone, where it remained for some time.

High jinks over, I wanted to proceed to the next stage. I had flirted with doing a Master's Degree and indeed was accepted to do something on the whole area of communication. It is one of the most important things that clergy do and yet sometimes we do not do it very well. I remember my father telling me at the Mission Hall one day that a guest preacher noticed there was a fellow sleeping during his sermon. He indicated to another person sitting in the pews that he should waken the sleeper. The person just said, 'you waken him, you put him to sleep.'

It has been my experience that many of the clergy speak too long, and I have probably been guilty of this.

Mark Twain remembers listening to a minister. He was very impressed and decided when the plate came round he would give him all his money. As he went on, Twain decided he would keep the notes and give the loose change. As he droned on even further, Twain decided that he would give him nothing. Eventually, when the sermon was over and the plate came round Twain took two dollars out - for spite! This helped me decide that effective communication should be my thesis. However, one morning I awoke and thought, enough of this. Being in the 'cloisters' was a wonderful experience, but it was time to get out into the real world and earn my living. I indicated to the church offices that I was ready for the next step.

I was subsequently told that I would be farmed out to a supervisor. It was suggested that I attach myself to the Rev Peter Houston, who was minister at Renfrew Old Church. I knew Peter from my Youth Fellowship days. He used to do a wonderful talk on Church music. It was a very special man who could enthuse a bunch of teenagers with the topic of Church music, but Peter did it. His talk was illustrated by his great ability as a jazz pianist and a group of well-chosen choristers often accompanied him. They gave it their all and I still recall him having 100 plus youngsters rolling in their seats, laughing, singing and clapping. Peter had us in the palm of his hand. I was keen to join him. Mind you, the grapevine information was that I should avoid Renfrew Old Church, as the minister was a hard taskmaster.

I did not find him so. He was fair and never asked me to do anything he was not prepared to do himself. He had a thing about visitation and every Sunday night you got a list of folk to visit, a huge list, a list of at least 30 names. I was expected to work my way through them all - and in the main, I did. He expected a report on every visit. He had cards printed for me, which said something like, 'Rev Ian Miller called today and found you out.' There was a bit of truth in that. Sometimes, I must confess, I would see someone down the street in Renfrew, hale and hearty and I would take the opportunity of nicking back to his or her address and putting a wee card through the door. Another one ticked off the list! In fairness, Peter believed it was a good way to get to know people, their problems, and hopes and indeed to share something of their lives. In the early years at Bonhill, I put his theory into practice and it worked.

On the 7th July 1974, I mounted the pulpit at Renfrew Old to preach my first sermon as the Rev Ian Miller (having been licenced to preach by the Presbytery of Paisley a few days earlier in Paisley Abbey). I remember the date vividly. Given the choice, I would have been elsewhere for it was the final of the World Cup, a great match that West Germany won, defeating Holland 2-1. I missed it, but I was off and running. I was a minister.

I had a happy time in Renfrew. I met some great people who confirmed my belief that the strength of the Church is more the people in the pews than in the pulpit. I remember there was a man who would always be there at the evening service then run (literally) to check on his elderly mother before returning home. That man was Jackie Husband, a faithful servant of the Church and of Patrick Thistle football club. I always think of him when I see his name emblazoned on the stand at Firhill that was named after him. A true gent and a true Christian.

Home life was great. Son Derek was growing and he brought so much joy into our lives. Whatever faults I may have, and I have many, I am so glad that as a father I was able to spend so much time and energy with the boys. It has been one of life's great privileges.

However, as my time at Renfrew ended I began to look around for my first parish. I had a fervent hope that it would be near Kilbarchan, which for Joan and I was the centre of our universe. That is where our parents lived and where almost all of our friends were. So where to go? That was the problem. There was nothing on the horizon.

Then, quite out if the blue, Bonhill came up.

It was a bit away but I did remember those cycle jaunts of my youth so I applied. Strangely, I never got a reply, and in the meantime, a church in Kilbirnie became vacant. I thought - 'Fine'. After all, Kilbirnie was nearer than Bonhill.

Though the congregation had not yet started looking for their new minister, I reckoned when they did it would be a sure thing.

What confidence and what arrogance! Then, one Sunday morning, just before going into the pulpit, Peter Houston indicated that a delegation from Bonhill were there to hear me preach. My response was that they were wasting their time as I had decided that I was going to Kilbirnie. End of story.

That afternoon, the Rev John Waddell who was Bonhill's interim Moderator, phoned me and asked me would I be prepared to be part of a short-list of three. I said that there was no point. I was going to

Kilbirnie. Within 10 minutes, John was back on the phone. The short-list of three was no more. The two other people had a church and so there was only me. Would I come and speak to the good folk of Bonhill? I indicated that it would be a waste of time. I was going to Kilbirnie, but John persisted. 'Give them a chance,' he said, and with great reluctance, I agreed. I reckoned it would be a good experience. It would be a dry run for Kilbirnie. In the month of April 1975, I made the journey to Bonhill.

I arrived at the church hall, which was demolished in the late 80s. I remember looking around while the church committee met for a pre-meeting meeting. The hall had a run-down look. It was not inspiring and I thought to myself - the person who comes here will have his work cut out. I was ushered into the little meeting room and confronted by about a dozen faces. The fact that I had no intention of going to Bonhill made it easy. I was going to Kilbirnie. This meant I was bullish. I asked them a few questions about what they expected from their minister. They indicated if I could turn up on a Sunday, maybe attend to weddings and funerals and do the odd visit then they would be happy. Expectations were low and I thought I could just about meet them.

For any young minister going to their first charge there was one big issue that worried them. Would their wife have to be President of the Woman's Guild? It was an issue for me. Joan was 24, Derek was not yet 18 months and Andrew was on the way, so there was no way she would be the President and I told them so in no uncertain terms. At that moment there was a woman on the front row, resplendent in her fur coat (church halls can be cold places). She rose to her full 5ft.3in. stature and said, 'of course not, I am the President of the Guild.' I could have kissed her. Aye Peggy McIntyre was maybe the one that started to chip away at my decision that Kilbirnie was the place for me. As the inquisition drew to a close, John Waddell, who had chaired the meeting said, 'anyone with any questions for the minister?' From the back of the hall, John Beaton shouted, 'Aye! Have you any tickets for the International?' (Scotland v England). I was beginning to warm to these people, but still

Kilbirnie called. I left without looking at the church or the manse. There was no point in this. I was going elsewhere.

I returned home to Joan who was keen to know how I had got on. I gave her a rundown but still indicated that I was still going to Kilbirnie. However, the people in Bonhill were really good people. I could work with them. They were ordinary, with a sense of humour. Maybe even at that stage I was beginning to consider the possibility.

The following Saturday, Joan and her lifelong friend, Allison Thompson, set off to 'case the joint'. They arrived at the church and were walking around when the church officer appeared. He saw these two longhaired, mini-skirted girls wandering round and invited them into the church. He explained there was to be a wedding later but he was keen they should see the place. He had no idea who they were and they were not for telling. Davie Kilpatrick's welcome and helpfulness impressed Joan and Allison and they came back enthused. Therefore, having seen neither the house nor the church, I agreed to go to Bonhill - a decision I have never regretted. My first experience of the warmth, acceptance and sheer good-natured humour of the Vale folk has continued for over 40 years.

On Wednesday 6th August, in the year 1975, I was ordained and inducted into the Parish of Bonhill. The 36th minister in a line that stretches back to 1458. A parish that can trace its history back to the monks of Paisley Abbey who were granted the fishing rights at the Linnbrane Pool on the River Leven. Little did I think I would become the second longest serving minister in a nearly 600-year history. The sermon centred on a verse from Paul to the Corinthians. The essence of which was, 'There's far more here than meets the eye. The things we see now are here today, gone tomorrow. But the things we can't see now will last forever.'

As Iain Galbraith, in his history of the parish, said - it would be my task to point people to the 'unseen realities'. The things that last forever.

That night would be well remembered by my many relatives who rhapsodised over the wonderful home baking of the Bonhill congregation. I remembered it for another reason. On leaving the church my Dad was quite emotional, finding it difficult to speak. He was probably having difficulty in understanding the daft laddie who burned down the aircraft hangar and who clowned his way through school would become a parish minister.

A 'Welcome Social' was held in the church hall the following night. Presentations were made and the Rev Robert Patterson, the minister at Jamestown Church, the man they called the Happy Padre of the Sunday Mail, made a hilarious speech. Bob was to become a good friend, but that night he had the audience in the palm of his hand. He lived up to his Happy Padre nickname. At one point Joan nudged me and said, through her laughter and clutching the 'bulge'; 'if that man does not stop then I can see me landing in Paisley Maternity tonight.'

The custom in those days was that on your first Sunday you did not preach. I asked the Rev Andrew Kerr, my parish minister from Kilbarchan, to 'preach me in'. I am glad I did. On the Friday night before that, my Dad and I had arranged a game of tennis at the public courts in Johnstone. He picked me up, we played the game. He dropped me off at the house. I jumped over a wall and landed on a spike, which pierced the tennis shoe and injured my foot. This meant that on Sunday the 10th August 1975, on my first appearance at Bonhill, I walked in, heavily bandaged and wearing slippers. I must have cut a great figure with the old folk wondering what they had been landed with.

Something interesting happened that Sunday morning. Unbeknown to me, Joan and parents were sitting fairly near the front. Behind them were three ladies of indeterminate age. One reached over and said to my mother in law, 'You will be very happy here.' My mother in law, Lizzie Parr was a real lady and she just nodded and smiled in response. Then another tap on the shoulder. 'When will you be moving through?' (The manse was still not ready for us). At this point realising mistaken identity Lizzie said, 'I am not the minister's wife.' Pointing to Joan, she said, 'she is.' A head poked further forward and Joan was scrutinised, the mini skirt and long hair noted and as the head withdrew she said to

Lizzie, 'aye a thought you were a bit too auld fur him but she is just a wee lassie'

The manse was in a state of disrepair that meant for me it was a commute from Johnstone to Bonhill every day and in the evening helping the members of the congregation to make the manse habitable. They soon realised that I was not gifted in the DIY stakes. Indeed, my father in law, who often came over to help, indicated to the members of my new congregations that I was a 'waste of space.' Best idea was to give me a paintbrush and tell me to paint the inside of the cupboards. This I did, managing to have the paint dripping down the paintbrush onto my arm and off my elbow onto the floor. Eventually the job was done -- and the manse was ready for its new occupants. We moved in at the beginning of November 1975, a very heavily pregnant Joan, Derek and me.

Her second pregnancy was not half as bad as the first but she still managed to spend a considerable time in hospital initially with the same sickness that had plagued her throughout her first pregnancy, and then later with hyper tension. In November they took her into the RAH in Paisley and kept her in.

I remember the day Andrew arrived. I can tell you exactly where I was when he entered this world. It was not holding my wife's hand, but conducting a wedding at Luss Parish Church. I missed the whole thing.

Doubtless you will wonder what happened to the 'alligator' that had returned to Thomson Avenue, Johnstone, on the night of the final year dinner. Well it also made the trip across the Erskine Bridge to Bonhill. As the removal men were moving the stuff into the manse, unknown to me, they had taken the alligator out and placed it quite near the semi derelict old garage. They then half covered it with leaves and as the children made their way home from the nearby Bonhill Primary school, they shouted them over. They then told the kids, 'look what just crawled out the River Leven.' The water was less than 100 yards away and the kids fled in fright.

It did come in handy as a prop in one or two talks I gave to the children but eventually, under pressure from Joan, I was instructed to get rid of it. I sold it to a television props company in Kilbarchan. The alligator was even featured in Scotland Today. Such fame! Now the real work was about to start ...

CHAPTER FOUR

THE CHURCH – THE EARLY YEARS

I was settling in, beginning to get to grips with Bonhill Church and the people. First impressions of their friendliness and openness were being confirmed. One Sunday morning as I was welcoming the congregation at the front door I said, 'Welcome Mrs Brown.' (In this instance, I have changed the name). 'How are you today?' Quick as a flash came the response, 'Nane the better for seeing you.' I think it was then I realised that not everyone was enthusiastic with the new young minister. I was determined to win her over and made a fair effort. I felt I was winning. One afternoon her district elder came to see me and said, 'I called on Mrs Brown today.' During his visit she had asked his opinion of 'that wan doon the road.' He indicated that I was 'not bad'. She retorted that I was simply a 'nyaff'. That word has stuck with me throughout my ministry. It was there when I was privileged to meet government ministers, speak at the Scottish Parliament, when I have married celebrities and served on the Health Board, at the end of the day there has been an inner voice keeping me humble with those words of Mrs Brown, 'Just remember you are just a nyaff.'

I eventually won her over - I think. Later in life, into her nineties, she was hospitalised and spent some considerable time in the Vale Hospital. I visited her regularly and one day she reached over and took my hand and said, 'We had some great times together.' I often wonder did I win her over, was she losing the place, or was it mistaken identity?

I have never been afraid of speaking my mind or challenging authority. Within months of being inducted, I fell foul of the Presbytery Clerk (Presbytery Clerks being the administrative official of the Presbytery, which in our case was at that time a collection of around 40 churches in the old Dumbarton County). The Moderator of the General Assembly was visiting the local area and the Council decided to accord him a Civic Reception. His visit coincided with a difficult time for the local authority and they had just announced cutbacks in the home help service. I felt there was something not right about this at a time when vital services were being curtailed. It was an opinion I might never have expressed had one of the local journalists not phoned me on some other issue, but causally asked would I be attending the reception. Not for the first nor last time my mouth was in gear before my mind and I indicated I would not be there and that I felt civic extravagance at this time was inappropriate. I suppose I saw it as a 'give away comment' in answer to a casual question. The local press however, took up the comment then the national press with lurid headlines.

Unbeknown to me the telephone lines between the Presbytery Clerk and the Church offices at 121 George Street, Edinburgh, were hot and shortly after that, so was my ear. I received a verbal ear bashing from the Clerk who tried to tell me, in the Queen's absence, the Moderator of the Kirk was the most important person in Scotland. That I did not believe then or now. Even if I had, I was for sticking to my position that the Kirk should be saying 'No' to civic expenditure at a time when local government was being forced to reduce the level of care to the needy. I was then told that expenditure would come from the Common Good Fund. On hearing this, well known journalist Bill Heaney wrote, 'If that is the case it's time some commoners got some good out of it.'

A few months before my arrival, the congregations of Bonhill South Church and Bonhill Old had united. I had been warned that getting the two congregations to work together would be a problem. It never was. The folk from the South Church had lost their beloved building, but they threw their heart and soul into making the union work. It became obvious this new congregation was very keen to be open and welcoming to all. How did they feel about me marrying anyone who was not a member of the church? Their answer was simple, 'They will never become involved in the church if we turn them away.' It was the same with baptism, funerals, use of the premises and from that simple philosophy of being open and accepting, things began to happen. The pews began to fill. It did not please everyone. When I indicated to one church member, it was good to see, her reply was, 'those now filling the pews are not real Christians.' I do not know how she knew. I may have got the Bible wrong but I do not ever remember Jesus turning people away. He had time for people, and mixed with sinners. I knew that in Bonhill, if I was to follow his example, I was going to have no problem finding sinners. If people wanted to have their child blessed, I blessed them. When you reject a child, you reject a whole family. I did not reject one.

The Sunday School was thriving and the Youth Fellowship was growing with a group of wonderful young people, many of whom were to become our baby sitters and friends. They were opinionated, challenging and a delight. Many of them are still involved in the present Kirk Session. Peter McDonald and Peter Nimmo became ministers. Ivan Coyle worked with the Church for a while and Gordon Yeaman was our organist. He brought along his girlfriend, Marion, and sister, Isobel, to sing in the choir and so the choir began to take on a new and younger look. Gordon was a character. He was in his late teens at the time and for the first few months he would turn up on Sunday morning, neatly dressed, white shirt, tie and suit. As time wore on and we became pals he said to me, 'Ian, do I need to dress up like this for Sunday?' I indicated it was a matter of little concern to me as to how he dressed. Indeed, I used the phrase if he came in his pyjamas it would not be a problem. He took me at my word. Sartorially there was a steady deterioration in standards, which did not go unnoticed at a time in the mid-seventies, when folk still preferred 'Sunday Best'. It became a matter of debate at the Kirk Session. I should have been brave and just said 'mea culpa' but I didn't. I did say I would speak to him, but I did not. One of the elders volunteered to do what I was reluctant to do. Panic seized me because I knew what would happen. Gordon, never reluctant to state his case, would have just blamed me for the fact that suit, tie and shirt had been binned. Eventually I said what I should have said from word go. 'Look, we have a great organist, a young and talented lad who has brought much to the church and he sits behind the organ console and nobody sees him, let sleeping dogs lie.' We did and were much blessed by Gordon's contribution until he and Marion were married and they took off to Shetland where their teaching and inspirational skills were a blessing to the young folk of that island.

I have many memories of Gordon. He had an ability to appear at my door at any time day or night. One night he arrived at 2am. I was sleeping, but the sound of little stones being thrown at the bedroom window quickly banished slumber. There was Gordon and he just wanted a blether.

We spent a few days playing golf together on the Solway coast, and staying at my folk's caravan. I had an attack of what I now presume was haemorrhoids. I had not been bothered before nor since with this but my nether regions were assailed by this incredible itch. In the darkness, I rummaged about the medicine cabinet and chanced upon a tube of cream which I liberally applied to the affected area. It got warmer and warmer until I felt I was on fire. What I thought was Germolene turned out to be Deep Heat, a mistake I would never make again.

My main thrust in those early years was to get to know the congregation. I visited diligently, listened to stories of aches and pains, complaints about the Church, criticism of my predecessors and of me. I listened attentively to an endless cataloguing of medical symptoms and began to think I might open a clinic in my spare time. I remember one occasion where this middle-aged woman gave me a blow-by-blow account of her symptoms and the eventual decision by the medical team to perform a hysterectomy. Nothing was omitted in this graphic description. My legs were firmly closed. She finished by saying, 'it has been so good to talk to you. I couldn't have done this if you had been a man.' I don't know what she thought I was, hermaphrodite perhaps? I wandered out of the hospital bemused.

LP cover of The Concords – Scottish Gospel group.   The church embarks on a 300k makeover.

The River Leven winds past Bonhill Church before the Glebe Estate was built...

In discussion with John Chalmers and Donald McQuarrie.   The only way is UP!

The Queen meets Ian (also known as St Barchan) on the Steeple Steps - Kilbarchan

In the late Seventies we decided we would stage a Gala Day in the church grounds, and so the tradition of the annual May Fair developed. It happened on the last Saturday of the month. We had decorated floats leaving the Ladyton car park and the procession that followed wound its way down to the churchyard where stalls were set up. It was a wonderful day and the community responded by giving its support.

The young folk got involved and often hired costumes. One year in particular we a wonderful assortment of lions, ostriches, penguins, bears, tigers and a gorilla made their way through the streets. The gorilla was Peter McDonald (now the leader of the Iona Community). He terrified the weans by running into the crowd as if to attack. I was persuaded to wear a chicken outfit so I 'cluck clucked' down the road. As we entered the churchyard one of the more sober members of the church looked directly at me and said, 'is it not time you grew up?' Succinctly I answered, 'Naw.' When you lose that child-like part of you, you have lost something significant. I hope I never do. Someone once said to me, 'Do we stop playing because we grow old or do we grow old because we stop playing?' I go for the latter.

Over the years, we were able to build some wonderful topical creations to lead the procession. Some of the senior members of the congregation, with construction and shipbuilding experience, got heavily involved in those projects. They worked in secret behind the closed doors of the now redundant South Church. The film Jaws was breaking box office records at the time and so they created a realistic 20-foot shark, which weighed in at three quarters of a ton. Another memorable creation was a life size space capsule - and with Ally McLeod giving strong indication that Scotland was going to win the world cup in 1978, the men built a ship to out-rival the Vital Spark as the 'smartest boat in the trade'. I think the intention was to use the vessel to transport Ally's army to Argentina.

Eventually the South Church and halls were demolished but not before someone stole the church bell from the crumbling 60-foot spire. A local scrap merchant indicated the bronze bell would be worth somewhere between £500 and £750, which was a lot of money in the late 70's. Indeed, at that time the church suffered a lot of from vandalism and theft. Windows were often a target, lead from the roof, brass fittings from inside the church, but then it all stopped, not immediately, but it stopped. I am not sure why but would like to think the more I got involved in the school, the more church doors were opened to community groups, the more hatches, matches and dispatches that took place within it, that all this made people feel Bonhill Church was their church. By the Eighties, right through to the present day, vandalism and theft has been almost non-existent.

When Derek and Andy were growing up, summer holidays were spent at my parents' caravan at Gatehouse on Fleet, then later around the Lake District or Scarborough.

The old manse had a lot of space, which the boys loved, and no central heating, which we hated. We endured one particularly bad winter in the late Seventies and Joan and I became hoarse shouting at the boys to close the door when they came into the living room to conserve heat. The church was keen to replace the manse. We could sell the Glebe land which belonged to the church and build a new house. The national church, however, is never good at moving things quickly and it is fair to say life was not easy. Strangely enough, it never affected the boys. Often their bedroom windows were frosted up (on the inside) yet they suffered from very few colds or bugs. I think at times it got to Joan. I was unaware at that time, but the Very Rev John Chalmers, who later became the Moderator of the General Assembly, and was minister at Renton, having concern for Joan, actually wrote to Killearn Church who were vacant at the time and suggested they might consider me. He never got a reply to his letter and though I was unaware of it, I am glad he did not. Things soon moved on. The head office in Edinburgh agreed to a scheme whereby the old manse and the Glebe were sold. The purchase price was to be a new manse and a sum of money. In June 1982, we moved into a new purpose built manse, centrally heated and with all mod cons.

At the same time, Eddie McMurray built eight rather nice pseudo Georgian terraced houses on the old South Church site. With their distinctive bow windows, they brought a bit of class to Main Street, Bonhill. Early in the building process, there was one amusing incident. Eddie had dropped in to have me sign some papers late one night, and as I pored over them, there was a disturbance outside in the Main Street. We looked out of the window and the scene before us was a full-blown 'domestic'. It caused us to take action and move quickly to intervene.

One of the travelling community had lifted a large stick from the building site and was using it to lay into his wife. Eddie and I raced to the scene. Eddie grabbed the wooden baton from the man's hands as I tried to shield the poor woman. However, with the stick rescued, Eddie crossed the road towards me. At that point the man, not happy his weapon had been taken from him, lifted up a large stone and threw it at Eddie striking him in the small of his back. Enraged Eddie took off in pursuit. This time he was brandishing the large piece of timber and managed to land his size tens on the poor man's nether regions. The man's shouts of anguish were heard along Main Street as he ran to escape retribution pleading for peace and calm. Those fell on deaf ears as the man dodged behind the nearest lamppost which Eddie began to strike repeatedly while the man shouted 'And you a man of God.' Eddie quickly disabused him of that perception with language, which as a cleric, was beyond my comprehension! At that moment, a passing car screeched to a halt an off duty police officer emerged to try to re-establish sanity. Neighbours by this time had alerted the police and it was not long before the sound of sirens announced their arrival. Eddie by this time was in the grip of the off duty police officer while I tried to explain to him what happened. The man of law was not for listening and cast me aside. The tinker was taken into custody and it appeared Eddie was to follow him. Thankfully, explanations were eventually accepted. The off-duty police officer was later to become a friend many years down the line.

One spectacular minus came when I was still living at the old South Church manse. I became concerned about an elderly member of the congregation whose mental faculties were declining and who, in my opinion, was beginning to be a danger to herself and to others. I broached the subject with her son and daughter-in-law. The daughter-in-law was an overpowering individual whose garish application of makeup would have done credit to Jezebel. She was concerned about her mother-in-law but her solution to the problem and mine were quite different. I think there may have been concerns if the old woman was taken into care then that the nest egg, which would in due course fall to them, might be considerably diminished. They did, however, conclude that I might be some sort of an ally in getting mum accommodated at minimal cost. Accordingly, they would descend on us usually at teatime. This was becoming an almost nightly occurrence.

One night, seeing their car drawing up at the manse, I shouted to Joan 'I am not in, get rid of them,' and bounded upstairs. I tried to listen to the conversation at the back door and was waiting for the sound of their departure. Instead, I heard Joan bringing them into the hall and living room. This was the last thing I wanted. Five, ten, fifteen minutes passed and then I heard Derek (probably at this time around age three) clambering upstairs. I could not let him see me. His shouts of 'Daddy' would be a sure giveaway. I went into the children's playroom, shut the door, and hoped he would go back down the stairs. He did not. He was a child on a mission and he energetically pushed at the door desperate to enter his domain. My back was against the door on the other side and I was equally determined he would not enter. Eventually, in disgust, I heard the child's footsteps retreating down the stairs with his plaintiff cry of 'door stuck.'

Time was moving on. I was hoping for something to eat before attending a Kirk Session meeting but how was I to get rid of my uninvited guests. I decided I had to get out of the house then re-enter in a way that would indicate I was a man in a hurry. How could I do that? Could I risk creeping downstairs with the possibility that Derek, still wishing to get into the playroom, would see me and give the game away? I could not risk it. Each of the main reception rooms had a bay window. I decided I would creep out one of the windows, grab a downpipe and lower myself the six or eight feet to the ground. One of the rooms we used as the living room, the other as a sort of reception room for folk who came to see me. I concluded that Joan would take them into the living room area. I clambered out on to the roof of the bay window to swing onto the down pipe hoping I had chosen the right room. If I had chosen the wrong one my uninvited guests would have had plenty to talk about seeing me, Tarzan like, lowering myself down to ground level. Thankfully, I had chosen correctly and breezing into the house, as if I had just come in with appropriate haste, I was able to usher them out. Otherwise, I think they were there for the night.

We were used to coping with uninvited guests. It was not unusual for me to return home and for Joan to be hosting a 'soup kitchen'. The travelling community were regulars. The usual story was that they were on their way to Perth and had just run out of diesel. Could they have a fiver? Perth for some reason was a favourite destination. Eventually I got into the habit of saying, 'a fiver will get you nowhere. Give me two minutes I will grab a jacket and take you to Perth.' That was usually the beginning of the end of our discussion. Joan, however, used to worry that they would call my bluff one day and say, 'fine.' It never happened.

It was about this time that I got involved in providing a chaplaincy service for Butlin's holiday camp in Ayr, a sort of ecclesiastical 'Hi-de-Hi. It was fun. I arranged that there would be a Church of Scotland minister on site for the entire season. I used to do a couple of weeks every year. Butlin's provided the chaplain with a chalet for his or her family and meals three times a day. You were expected to take two services every Sunday, be on call 24/7 and attend to any pastoral problems. Additionally, we judged the Bonnie Babies, Lovely Legs and Glamorous Grannies. After about 12 years of this Butlin's suspended operations at Ayr. It was fun while it lasted.

Also at that time, my parents left Kilbarchan and came over to live in the Vale. We acquired a piece of ground on Queen Street, Alexandria, and built a three-bedroomed bungalow. Again, Eddie McMurray and his two sons did a wonderful job and Mum and Dad moved to Alexandria. They named their new house 'Derand', (unimaginatively using the first three letters of both their grandchildren's names).

They had 14 happy years in Queen Street. Ernie Miller became fully involved in the church, helping at the organ now and again. Every Sunday he and I would go into Dalreoch House in Dumbarton, (a care home) and conduct a service. He playing the organ and leading the singing and me taking the short service. We did this for many years. He also became a member of the Kirk Session. Probably after his Mission Hall days, it was a bit of a culture shock, but he coped. Indeed, after his first Easter, when he and I attended a dawn service on Carman Hill, he just said, 'That was the best Easter ever.' They were warmly embraced by the congregation and found the Vale of Leven to be everything I told them it would be. I suppose it is not easy when you move to a new location later in life but for them it was liberating. They were now near the grandchildren and, as Mum's arthritis took more of a hold, they brought her much joy. Her face would light up when the two boys, Derek and Andrew, popped over.

My zeal for the abolition of nuclear weapons involved me in some very heated debates on the floor of Dumbarton Presbytery and on the floor of the General Assembly. In the early days, the argument that possession of the nuclear bomb was a necessary evil often seemed to win. Possession was held to be both rational and moral. Then the tide began to turn. In a watershed moment, the General Assembly opposed Trident and has continued to increase its opposition to its replacement. In those early days, the Church and Nation debates at the General Assembly were probably the nearest Scotland got to its own parliament and they were followed with great interest. The level of debate was of the very highest.

At that time, it could have been said of our community that the three main providers of employment were makers of cameras, whisky and bombs. Polaroid was a big employer, J&B's Strathleven Bond and Allied Distillers sustained the local community. The nuclear bases at Coulport and Faslane provided work for countless people. I suppose it could have been argued that I was taking a risk of alienating the local community by threatening their livelihood. Some did debate the issue with me but others indicated they had to work and wished they could have found meaningful employment outwith the armament industry. Perhaps the most critical comment I ever had was from one of the MOD police who, as we neared the gates of Faslane in a protest march, shouted, 'Hey Miller, away and work.'

It was probably because of my involvement in CND that I was invited to take part in what was called the St Andrew's Day Debate in the early 1980s. It was produced by the BBC and hosted in the Royal College of Surgeons in Edinburgh. It was a two-hour programme produced by BBC, introduced by Ludovic Kennedy, and chaired by Ernest Armstrong MP. He was deputy speaker in the House of Commons. The UK government had just announced in 1980 that they intended replacing Polaris with the Trident missile system

Speaking for the retention of nuclear arms and supporting the decision to replace Polaris with Trident was Sir Anthony Heritage Farrar-Hockley GBE, KCB, DSO and Bar. At age 15, he ran away from school and joined up to serve in WW2. He had a very distinguished military career, ending as NATO's Commander in Chief.

There was also Lady Olga Maitland, a formidable woman who made Maggie Thatcher look vulnerable and Sir Geoffrey Johnson-Smith MP, who was proud of his Glasgow background. There are not too many hyphenated names in Glasgow. He was a defence specialist and a bit of a TV personality. Interestingly he did say both the Pope and the Archbishop of Canterbury of the time supported the possession of the nuclear deterrent. The present ones do not.

Gerald Warner was there, a journalist who never holds back on his opinions but an interesting person. I suspect I would agree with him on very little but find his opinions fascinating. The Rev William Morris who was at that time minister at Glasgow Cathedral woke up the invited audience when he asserted that the Bomb was a gift from God. The speaker who followed him was quite thunderstruck.

The other cleric was the Very Rev. Gordon Reid, who at that time was an episcopal cleric from Inverness. The tabloids later exposed his very irreverent activities. He left these shores in disgrace over alleged activities not regarded as consistent with the ministry. I believe he still plies his trade in the USA. Dr Gavin Kennedy of Strathclyde University and Marshall Harris of the United Nations were there.

On the other side was Monsignor Bruce Kent, leader of CND; Dr James Dyer, who was an expert on the medical effects of a nuclear war; Duncan Campbell a journalist; Donald Stewart MP, who at that time was the leader of the SNP; and Martin O'Neill. Martin was, at that time, an MP who vigorously opposed Trident and believed Scotland should be nuclear free. He is now Lord O'Neil of Clackmannan. I think as well as changing his title he has also changed his opinion on Trident.

It is interesting how folk like George Robertson, now of NATO, was once a card carrying CND supporter, and of course, Brian Wilson, the former MP, has changed his opinion. Mind you, Brian was good when he was with the Beach Boys! I suppose we can all change our minds. Either they learned sense, as some would say, or betrayed their political roots.

Making up the rest of the opposition bench was Kay Caldwell, of Parents for Survival; Dr Steadman, an expert on casualties, former Dumbarton District Councillor, Ian Leitch, and myself. It was a great night and summed up by Menzies Campbell for the anti-bombers, who I think has now also changed his mind, and Lord Mansfield, who spoke most eloquently for the retention.

However, for me the star performer was Ian Leitch, a former councillor, lawyer and formidable debater. Ian is articulate, amusing and passionate, and he was on top form that night. He listened to everyone and completely unscripted rose to speak. He had the audience in his hand and had the great gift of making them laugh.

To those who asserted possession of the bomb made the world a safer place and backed up this claim by reminding that there had been no nuclear war, Ian said that was like the fellow jumping from the 18th floor of a Glasgow high rise flat and as he passed the 12th floor shouting out, 'I haven't hit anything yet!'

He continued, 'If it does make the world a safer place then let's give everyone the bomb - give Galtieri (then President of Argentina) the bomb, give Gaddafi the bomb.' Even those who opposed him laughed.

To the good general who had indicated that, if anyone enters your home you have right to defend yourself and your family, Ian countered, 'Yes, but you do not blow the whole house up.'

His speech was a combination of humour and tongue in cheek comments, all in the best debating style. His opponents admired his wit and eloquence. There was no vote but it was compelling viewing. Maybe BBC should resurrect the concept now that Trident Mark 2 is an issue.

The thought of nuclear war is terror on a global scale but there are also other kinds of terror.

Neighbours are important in life and our Bonhill neighbours blessed us. We laughed with them and sometimes cried with them through life's difficulties. Stewart and Linda Brown lived across the road from us in Glebe Gardens. They are not related to that other 'Broon' family who live in Glebe Street. A happy family, but one day I shared their complete terror when their little daughter inexplicably vanished from the face of the earth. This is every parent's worst nightmare. Almost instantaneously, the whole neighbourhood was alerted. Gardens and garden sheds were searched. It was obvious that she was not in the house, which had been searched from top to bottom. The search began to widen, a number of spectres floated in our minds. Had she been abducted? She was a beautiful blue-eyed, blonde child of about three years of age. Part of me said this only happens to other people but still the thought would not go away. People became more worried and frenetic. The circles growing wider even down to the nearby River Leven. When do you suggest to parents that maybe we should be calling in the police? Meanwhile, our Andrew who often 'haunted' the Brown household, sharing an interest in cars, boats and gadgets with Stewart, returned to the house to look where everyone else had already looked. We continued the search outside.

As he was later to relate, as he searched fruitlessly throughout the house, looking in areas a little one might have strayed, and was about to rejoin us when he decided to have one last look in the playroom. There was no nook or cranny in which she could have hidden, but as he turned to leave, his eye caught the slightest movement in a pile of soft toys. He wondered if it was just his imagination but started forward and began to delve deeper into the pile. There sleeping peacefully, blissfully unaware of the panic she had caused, was Holly Brown.

Holly, by the way, is now a mother herself and living with the family in Orlando. I am sure if her child goes missing, the first place she will look is among the soft toys!

One similar incident remains in my mind. I had gone to Balloch along the towpath, which runs beside the River Leven with the two boys on their cycles. The Leven is the second fastest flowing river in Scotland. Only the Spey is faster. It flows eight miles from Loch Lomond past the communities of Balloch, Jamestown, Alexandria and Bonhill then twists and turns in a horseshoe loop past Renton, slowing down when it reaches Dumbarton and enters the Clyde at Dumbarton Rock. The river has been so important to our community in the past, bringing prosperity. The soft clear waters were ideal for the textile industry.

During the summer months, children would play on its banks and swim in its waters, but there was another side to it. Over the years, it has claimed many lives. On this particular Saturday, Derek had gone ahead of Andrew and myself on the return journey. Normally he would cycle a bit and then wait for us. On this occasion, he disappeared.

Andrew and I speeded up to catch up with him but to no avail. In my mind, there were two explanations. Travelling at speed, he could have skidded off the towpath into the Leven or had decided to make his way back to the manse. He had never done this before, but there is a first time for everything. With my heart in my mouth, I made my way home and shouted to Joan, 'Is Derek here?' The answer was, 'No.' Fear and apprehension had by this time taken hold. Another thought came to me. Was it possible he had made his way to his grandparents' house? This was almost instantly dismissed but it did seem a possible alternative to my worst fears. I ditched the bike, grabbed the car and sped over to Queen Street. I flew in the door dashed into the living room and, relief beyond belief, there was Derek sitting with his gran eating a morning roll

I often think of the story Jesus told about the boy who went off on a 'gap year'. When the daft laddie came to his senses and headed homewards after the money ran out and he had swapped gourmet cooking for pigswill, it is said his father was overjoyed. That was not my emotion. I felt relief, yes, but not joy. In fact, I do not think Derek was able to sit down for a week. My reaction then, which I regret, would have today prompted a call to ChildLine.

Living by the Leven, we were well aware of the river's ability to claim lives. On a number of occasions, I have stood on the windswept hill above the Valley intoning the words of committal as we lay to rest a loved one whose life had been forfeited to the river.

*

As time went on our holidays became more adventurous. We decided we would go abroad. I was not into flying so we trailed across Europe by car. Initially we went to France then later Switzerland, Austria, Germany and Italy. It was Euro Camping - a luxury update on what I had known as a teenager. The boys loved it. They met up with other kids and it used to amaze us how easily they were able to communicate with children whose language was not English. Sorry, I should say amazed that those children were able to understand *them*. 'Di ye want a game o' fitba?' does not easily translate into any other language but somehow it worked. Those were activity holidays and never a day passed where we were not up mountains, chair lifts, cable cars, funiculars or canoeing, white water rafting or hiking. Those were great holidays. The boys just loved them and so did Joan, as long as the sun was shining. Later on, we were able to take some of their pals. I have memories of being at the top of Gornergrat near the Matterhorn with Andy, Derek and Michael Jones. Snow was everywhere and I introduced the boys to Gluewein and Grog to heat them up. Not a good idea. High altitude and grog don't go well together.

By this time, the boys were at the senior school and badminton became their main interest. They played for both school and county, winning trophies for themselves and their teams. Undoubtedly, a huge influence on them both was the PE teacher Douglas Morrison. I wonder if teachers, youth leaders and sports coaches realise the huge influence they have on young lives for bad and good. Derek and Andy would have died for Dougie.

They both became involved in the school team and the county team, and on a Saturday, during term time, I became more and more of a taxi driver, ferrying children to such exciting places as Cumbernauld, Glenrothes, Grangemouth, Meadowbank and so on. We were not alone and so, along with the competitors there, we were the cheerleaders - the Youngs, the Laings, the O'Neils, the Smiths and many more. Campbell Smith is also one of those unsung heroes who, along with the Crook family, the Crawfords and others, have kept badminton alive in our community. Derek struck up a profitable doubles partnership with Craig Young, winning a Scottish doubles title at one stage. Off the court, there was another partnership - the late John Young and Ian Miller. We maintain we never lost a single match while sitting on the side-lines. It was great fun. Every lunchtime Dougie Morrison would have a group of youngsters in the school gym hall coaching and encouraging them.

As well as introducing them to the game of badminton, he inspired them, and I am quite convinced that his inspiration flowed into their academic studies. As a family, we felt we owed Douglas Morrison so much. Success on the court was wonderful, but it was a privilege to get to know so many wonderful young people. I remember, however, the expression on the faces of some of the parents from more illustrious schools as our minibus pulled away with Craig Young leading the singing of 'Keep the Vale Flag Flying High' (to the tune of the Red Flag). I must confess I also joined in.

After Douglas retired, I was privileged to enjoy many a game of golf with him and our mutual friend Stan Jones. Andrew joined us on quite a few occasions. He would refer to Douglas as 'Mr Morrison'. Dougie of course would say, 'Come on Andy, it is Dougie.' Andy would reply 'Yes, Mr Morrison.' He could not change the habits of a lifetime - a lifetime of respect. Dougie then decided that he would just call Andy, 'Mr Miller' and so it was. It was a sad day for us all when Douglas Morrison, a gentleman if ever there was one, was called from this scene.

On one occasion, Andy got through to the semi-finals of the Scottish Championship at his age group. He was forced to play on the main courts before quite an audience and later he was to say, "My legs were like rubber..." It is funny how the mind can affect the body. Nerves simply overcame him.

Another great influence on the boys was David Calder. He was also a character and inspiration. He taught Chemistry at the Vale Academy and both boys decided, after school, to study Chemistry at University.

Derek went to Strathclyde and Andy to the West of Scotland University in Paisley. They were offered places at Glasgow, but opted to go elsewhere - no class those boys.

During their later school years and early university, they supported themselves by doing a Sunday paper run. It was lucrative. Like a couple of Mafia dons they extended their territory and 'bought up' other smaller enterprises. Problem was, their delivery bags became so large and heavy they would have given Hercules a problem. So they employed a sleeping partner - ME. However, I was not really a *sleeping* partner. I used to get up while they slept, picked up the papers from the newsagents, sorted them out and then I delivered around one third of them to residences close to the manse. Mostly it was done in darkness. No one had any idea who was delivering their *Sunday Post*. I then returned, made their breakfast and acted as driver while they skipped over fences and hedges to deliver the news to the village of Bonhill. In the darkness, I put the final touches to the 'Good News' that I would later bring to the Bonhill congregation.

I realised my newspaper-delivery cover was broken when, after a Christmas Eve service, my nearby neighbour, Jackie Ryden, handed me a little present. It was a small ceramic plaque on which was a picture of a matchstick man, delivery satchel slung over his shoulder, with a halo on his head and the simple legend - *To Rev Ian Miller – 'Paper Boy of the Year' 1991-1992.*

*

Over the years, I had developed an irrational fear of flying. Indeed, I had not flown since around 1965. I was determined to conquer this fear and tried everything - psychotherapy, hypnotherapy, Diazepam, the power of prayer, even a half bottle of brandy. I reckon a combination of all five got me onto a plane in the mid-90s when I took part in an exchange with an American pastor by the name of the Rev Mansfield Kasemann, who was minister of Rockville URC Church in Maryland. Kasey, as he preferred to be called, and his wife Diane came to Bonhill and Joan, Derek, Andy and I went to Rockville, which was conveniently just outside Washington DC.

We received the most amazing reception from Kasey and Diane and indeed all the Rockville folk. On the night before he left for Bonhill Kasey asked me what he should wear and, in particular, he asked what preaching stole might be appropriate. He had so many! One caught my attention. It was green and white. I had to explain to him the whole

Rangers/Celtic thing and why I suggested that particular one. Well Kasey milked it for all he was worth. In typical American fashion, he told the good people of the Vale how it was so important he bonded with them. He had sought my advice as to what would be important and, with that, he produced the green and white preaching scarf and draped it over his shoulders. It is a long time since Jenny Geddes hurled her 'hymn book' at the preacher, so Kasey ran a big risk that Sunday, but it paid off. Bonhill took Kasey and Diane to their hearts. By the time he returned he had been 'converted' and was the proud possessor of about half dozen Rangers hats and scarfs.

We Millers enjoyed our month in the USA. We visited all the historic sites of the Washington area and even spent a week in Orlando enjoying the theme parks. That visit proved to me that you cannot go anywhere without being recognised. While enjoying the sights of Disneyland a woman screamed and then launched herself at me from the crowds. It was quite pleasant, but you do not expect one of your best friends to appear unexpectedly when you are thousands of miles from home. I still have visions of Allison Thompson's two boys, Paul and Steven, joining our two, singing *I would Walk 500 Miles*, in best Proclaimers style, always first up on the Karaoke.

Kasey had a house in West Virginia where we also spent some time. A little incident happened there, which gave me another insight into our transatlantic cousins. The boys and I were keen to play tennis. There was a tennis court at Kasey's complex. There were tennis rackets in the house but no tennis balls. We went down to a little sports shop in the nearby town of Hancock and walked into a veritable arsenal. Every conceivable type of lethal weapon was on display - shotguns, handguns and crossbows. There was enough to kit out an army. We asked the owner if he might have some tennis balls. After all, it was a 'sports shop'. He rummaged around at the rear of the shop and returned with four. In the meantime, smiling customers had left the shop clutching the armoury and munitions of a small country.

The people we met in America, almost without exception, were lovely, charming and hospitable. However, there is much about the country and its politics I do not understand, its gun laws being just one.

While in West Virginia the boys did a stint of white water rafting, down the Potomac, stopping at Harpers Ferry where the waters of the Potomac join those of the Shenandoah. They saw no sight of John Brown or his body.

This visit to the USA set in motion a series of visits and connections with Rockville. Some of their congregation came to Scotland and some of ours went to America. Many of the friendships established over 20 years ago continue to this day.

On one of our visits (just Joan and I this time) we flew out from Dulles Airport to Heathrow. Though flying had become a little easier, I was still not delirious about it. As we left Dulles, one of the flight attendants strapped herself in just across from us and engaged us in conversation. She was a pretty lass. We blethered away and before I knew it, we were up, up and away. Maybe that was the cure I had missed.

Later another of the girls came down the aisle to cater to our needs. She was Scottish and I asked her where she came from. Her answer was 'Glasgow'. She asked where I came from and when I said Bonhill she exclaimed, 'That's where my husband came from.' I then asked his name. On being told that it was Scott McHugh I then replied, 'I married you.' And indeed, I had. She then got us transferred to First Class and got us onto the flight deck. Indeed, I sat in the cockpit as we landed at Heathrow. It was quite an experience and sadly one other thing that was brought to an end by the tragedy of 9/11. As I remember that experience, I also remember that, tragically, Scott was also taken from us prematurely.

*

The dawning of 1986 allowed us to celebrate the 150th anniversary of the opening of the present church. It is interesting to note that shortly after its opening there was a lack of harmony among the notables (called *heritors*) of the parish. They were in the main the ones who had footed the bill for its construction.

My dear friend Dr Iain Galbraith, who has written a most masterly history of the church and parish, tells how there was a dispute about who was sitting where! In his words, *'There were some undignified manoeuvres to obtain rights to the front gallery pews - the acme of class distinction in the 19th century parish of Bonhill.'* In other words, the gentry claimed the best seats, the most prominent at the front of the gallery. As Iain puts it, *'A descending order in the House of God, there was also provision made for the poor, but not in the gallery.'*

The 150th anniversary was celebrated with a special service and pageant in front of the church, where we recreated some of the important moments in its long history and allowed some of the long-deceased ministers to have their 'say'.

The church was built in 1836 at a cost of £2,304 and could seat over 1000 people. Prior to the church of 1836, there had been other buildings on or around the same site. I hope that the present one will still be serving us when its 200th anniversary is reached in 2036. Its predecessor had a relatively short life. It was built in 1797 and needed to be replaced less than 40 years later. Apparently, the builders had made the mistake of building it too close to the River Leven and the foundations were adversely affected. The builders, and indeed the congregation, must have missed the story Jesus told of making sure your foundations are on rock, not on sand!

CHAPTER FIVE

CHALLENGES AND REBUILD

ONE of the major problems for any congregation is maintaining buildings. The old manse, our initial home, was fit for a day and time long since past. It was a good day when the congregation were able to acquire a new manse that would serve them well into the next century.

We then turned our attention to other problems. The church was built in 1836 and the halls later on in the same century. The latter in particular was showing its age. It was a shock, however, to discover the church building was also in need of major expenditure. The walls were moving outwards. It did not require a degree in building technology to realise that if the walls moved out the roof would fall in.

A building survey in 1985 indicated it would be necessary to spend over 100k to return the church building to its former glory. The office-bearers sadly concluded that it would be impossible to raise that sum and, with regret, they would have to leave their beloved building behind. The suggestion was made and accepted that we unite with the neighbouring Alexandria churches and that two ministers - Rev W.J.E. McFarlane and I - would staff the united church. It says much for the Bonhill congregation that they were prepared to go forward with this plan. The Presbytery, however, had a rethink. Bonhill was an expanding community and it was by far the largest centre of population in the Vale of Leven. It seemed like an admission of defeat to leave it without a church and so a new plan was developed.

Utilising the talents of three recently-ordained Auxiliary Ministers (non-stipendiary), we would recreate within the one building a sanctuary and a suite of halls. These three men were Bill McKay (a Partner in a Civil Engineering firm), Roy Wilson (who held a similar position in a firm of architects) and Harry Dutch (head of publicity for Strathclyde Council). Roy drew up a set of imaginative plans, Bill set about getting sponsorship and Harry started to raise the profile of the church and get press interest in our scheme.

The congregation embraced the project. Key figures emerged who, along with the above-named, would drive it to a successful conclusion. The Presbytery and The General Trustees of the Church of Scotland were supportive and planning for the undertaking got underway. It was a step of faith - even blind faith - as our collective assets did not amount to much.

People in the community offered to help in any way they could, members of the congregation rolled up their sleeves and this unique venture began to gather speed. Unique because projects of this nature would normally be handled and underwritten by professional bodies. Our scheme depended on the unpaid help and advice of Roy, Bill and Harry. It was important, however, that we would have a clerk of works who would supervise the day-to-day work. This was a cost we would have to bear - at least so we thought. At that moment, Arthur Menzies gave up his employment as Transport Manager with the Electricity Board. Stopping on the Friday, he took over as our unpaid clerk of works on the Monday. The debt of gratitude the congregation owed Arthur was immense. He was an inspiration, a friend and support to me when things were going wrong.

It became obvious that the congregation would have to find a temporary home while reconstruction took place. The initial plan was to take the building back to four bare walls and the earthen floor. We moved out of the church in the spring of 1987. At the end of a service one Sunday, we removed the communion table, font and lectern for storage, to be followed later in the week by every pew. During our exile from the church, those pews found rest in the bonded warehouse of Barton Distillery, their board and lodging provided gratis by managing director Mitchell Sorbie.

The following week we meet in Ladyton School. We were welcomed by the 'janny', Jack Melvin, who helped, Sunday by Sunday, to lay out the chairs. Remaining in order to hear the sermon, however, was a step too far for Jack.

Services in the school were different. They were held in the assembly hall and it was not unknown for the back doors to burst open during a service when there had been a baptism and for a taxi driver to shout, 'Taxi for Smith!' Of course, half the congregation would get up and leave. What was interesting was that people came along who had never entered the church building. It was fun and not without incident.

Eddie Coyle the Session Clerk and Davie Kilpatrick, our beadle, were always first to arrive and, along with Duncan McKinlay the treasurer, the last to leave. Eddie was an institution with some interesting verbal mannerisms peculiar to the Vale of Leven. He would often emphasise points he had to make by saying things like, 'Our service next week will be at 11am -- so it will.' Preparing for a forthcoming communion it was not unusual for him to say something like, 'Shiona McKay will be on the wine -- so she will.' A vision of Shiona under the influence of Buckfast would enter our consciousnesses. Eddie liked to prepare well for communion. The church was his domain. He would come over to the church on Saturday morning and have everything laid out. He did not have this luxury at Ladyton - what had to be done had to be done quickly, so it was no surprise that now and again there would be a mishap. Just as I began the service one Sunday, he muttered into my ear, 'There's nae wine in the goblets.'

'Where is it?' I asked.

'In the classroom,' was the reply.

'Then get it,' I instructed.

I decided to play for time. During a long entreaty to the Lord, I could hear Eddie returning to the assembly hall while at the same time pouring the wine into the chalice. The glug, glug, glug was heard by the entire congregation. I say wine...in fact it was not wine. Early on, it was decided we should not use alcoholic wine. This followed an appeal from

Alcoholics Anonymous that we should not put temptation in the way of those recovering from addiction. Accordingly, we used some sort of substitute. Usually that substitute was unfermented grape juice. On one occasion, however, the issue was raised at our monthly Session Meeting by one of the senior elders, Jimmy Lappin. He was a character. A former SAS commando, when he had something to say he was going to say it. So he posed the question: 'At the last communion, whit was the wine we used?'

Quickly I answered, 'Jimmy it would be the unfermented grape juice.'

Jimmy was not to be deterred. 'Naw, it wisnae.'

'Yes Jimmy,' I assured him, 'IT WIS!'

Meanwhile, Eddie had been trying to say something and eventually he got his chance. He said, 'Naw it wisnae. It wis the Ribena so it wis.'

It was not to be the only occasion on which Jimmy won a verbal joust. Arriving a little late for a Session Meeting, I explained the reason for my delay. I had been visiting Eddie Jones' (not his real name) widow, for Eddie had died suddenly.

Jimmy said, 'Naw.'

I was mystified. What was his problem? I knew where I had been - I had been visiting the deceased's widow. I re-stated what I had been doing.

Again, Jimmy just said, 'Naw.'

Eventually I said, with some exasperation, 'Jimmy what's your problem?'

'No widow - just 'bidey in'.'

Again, I had egg on my face.

Ladyton School was a liberating experience. I am sure we thought our exile would be fairly short - somewhere between 6 and 9 months as Bill McKay's sponsorship deals kicked in saving us huge sums of money.

Sadly, we were to be dealt a huge blow when Bill announced the break-up of his marriage and his resignation from the ministry. He had moved out of the family home he shared with his wife, Chris, and was involved in a new relationship. Bill was held in high esteem at Bonhill and this revelation came as a great shock. It was also a surprise for us to discover that, for reasons we were never able to ascertain, the promised sponsorship was not going to materialise. This was perhaps the lowest moment of the venture. A possible bill of £100k had now rocketed to £300k. We faced four bare walls, an earthen floor, and, it seemed, no way forward. However, Roy Wilson, along with Arthur Menzies, remained convinced that we would see it through. Into the situation came Eddie McMurray, who promised to do as much as he could for cost! A number of community enterprises agreed to donate time if we paid for the materials.

Members of the congregation came together twice a week to offer help. A project group was set up to monitor progress and Arthur was ever-present.

There was one thing Arthur and some of the volunteers disagreed upon. The volunteers wished to demolish the huge horseshoe gallery that went round three walls of the church. Arthur decreed it was too dangerous and must go out to contract. Though he was usually there to direct the efforts of the volunteers, one evening he took the night off.

That was the night we decided to take action. With the uninhibited glee of school children when the teacher is absent, we set about the demolition of the gallery. More than at any time, the image of that night is imprinted on my memory. Grown men given permission to be vandals. Bob Johnstone hauling the front of the gallery back and forward till it gave way and crashed down. It was a great night. We attacked the structure with vigour and by the end of the night the entire gallery structure had been dropped to the floor below. We had done the job. No contractor would be needed. At that moment, when there should have been jubilation, a strange mood came over the assembled volunteers. In their minds was the unspoken word... ARTHUR!

It was decided we would keep out of his road for a few days, but the following morning he appeared and had a look at the scene. It resembled the Clydebank Blitz. He was silent for a few minutes, then he took two large pieces of wood and nailed them across the entrance to what had been the gallery to prevent further access, His only comment was, 'I presume Action Man was here last night.' That comment was taken to be a reference to me. I stayed out of his way for a week and the incident was never mentioned, however it further added to Arthur's opinion that I might have my uses but they were to be confined to spiritual rather than practical exercises.

One of the big controversies related to the church organ. It was agreed that the old organ, built in 1882 at a cost of £408, should be replaced. It was obvious that there were two camps: those in favour of a pipe organ, the others for an electronic or digital organ. Initially it appeared the pipe organ would win. We received some great advice from Dr Iain Galbraith, whose family had a long and distinguished connection with Bonhill Church. He and others earmarked the Lammermoor hand-built Pipe Organ as the ideal replacement. The cost would be about £25k. A delegation travelled to Altringham to hear the organ and returned impressed. There is nothing to compete with a good pipe organ, but it comes with a price. It must be continually looked after, like a vintage car. However, the alternative - the digital computer organ - was gaining favour. It would be almost maintenance free. It was agreed we should arrange a demonstration of the Allen Digital Computer Organ.

It was a lovely summer evening and the church was full, some believing no electronic organ could compete with the 'real thing', others hoping it might prove to be the cheaper, more versatile option. The demonstration began and, for most folk, the sound was 'jaw-dropping'. The variety of sounds and the purity of sound were impressive. A true musician like my friend Iain Galbraith would detect a difference but we suspected the vast majority of the congregation would welcome the variety of sound and versatility that the Allen could offer. It also helped that our organist, Andrew Lockhart, was in favour of the Allen.

There are two little postscripts to the story.

Firstly, one of the local GPs (also a pipe organ enthusiast) was sure we were making the wrong decision. A member of the congregation had gone for a consultation and the doctor had patiently taken time to explain the benefits of a 'real pipe organ'. The dialogue had taken 30 minutes. At the end of it, having dealt with the medical issue, the patient bid the doctor farewell and then said, 'Doctor, you are going to have to get me out by the back door, for if I have to go through that waiting room, having kept everyone waiting, they will presume I have something either life threatening or highly contagious.' And so Davie Thompson slipped quietly and unseen out of the surgery via the rear exit.

The other issue was paying for the new organ. Eddie McMurray had a meeting with the businessman Sir Hugh Fraser, whose House of Fraser group had just been sold to the Fayed brothers. When Eddie mentioned the Bonhill project, Sir Hugh took a chequebook from his pocket and wrote a cheque to Bonhill Church for £10,000. When replying, I thanked him and indicated it would go towards the purchase of our new organ. Two days later, Sir Hugh phoned me and asked what the total cost of the organ would be. I told him that it would be £25,000. Very briefly, he said there would be another cheque in the post for £15k. True to his word, it arrived. Sadly, it would be one of the last cheques he ever wrote. A few days later, he slipped from this world. The Allen organ, which was bought almost 30 years ago, has in that time given the church wonderful and trouble-free service.

Having expected to be out of the church for around six months, our exile to Ladyton School was to last nearer three years; however, they were wonderful years, full of excitement and laughter. As a congregation, we came together in a way that might not otherwise have been possible. It was not, however, without disasters.

With the promised sponsorship not having materialised we were forced to do much of the work ourselves, helped by Furnish Aid and Community Industry. The latter group was a job creation exercise employing young people on a short-term basis, giving them experience of work. It would be true to say not all were 'angels' and now and again things would go missing! Arthur decided to tackle the issue. He had a showdown meeting with the kids and their supervisors, indicating, as only Arthur could, that the thieving had to stop.

He obviously got through to them. He had some other business to attend to and left them to their own devices. When he returned the whole place had been transformed. He complimented them and asked where they had stored the organ pipes (these were the lead pipes from the old organ and worth a bit of money). No one seemed to know. At that moment, our self-appointed caretaker, Robin Stewart, was attempting to speak. Arthur, however, was not often inclined to listen to Robin's often long and convoluted stories. He dismissed his attempts as he tried to find out what had happened to the pipes. No one had an answer and eventually Arthur was mystified. Where had they gone? Robin took the opportunity to tell his story.

'As I was coming over Bonhill Bridge, I saw someone going in the opposite direction. He had a wheelbarrow and on it there seemed to be long cylindrical things. In fact, they looked like torpedoes.'

Robin had witnessed the removal of the organ pipes and had not raised the alarm. Arthur's response is unprintable.

There were very few break-ins at the church, which was indicative of the good relationship between church and community. However, there was one. There was minimal damage but a few items, albeit of little value, were taken. Arthur was annoyed. Why would someone do this to 'his church'?

Robin was keen to add to the investigation. Arthur was equally disinclined to hear his theory, but Robin waited for his moment and seized it. In his own inimitable, stuttering, long-winded way, he informed those of us present, 'I realised there was something wrong, something that was not right. As I went into the bell room I saw something on the floor that should not be there.'

I could see Arthur losing interest in the story, but Robin was working up to the punch line. He was having difficulty finding the right word for what he had seen on the floor. He paused, still searching. 'It was a...it was a...it was a...'

'It was a *what*?' exploded Arthur.

'It was a jobby!' concluded Robin.

It was quite usual for apprentice burglars to leave such a distinctive trademark behind.

As the project inched towards completion, the congregation and community were generous. Yet there were times when funds ran low. On one occasion, our treasurer indicated no more money should be spent on materials. Community Industry were providing the labour for free but we had to provide the materials needed. The following day Allan McKay, the supervisor, approached me about ordering wood. I explained our problem. He understood but indicated that if there were no materials they would probably have to move to another project. I decided to give the order the 'go-ahead', knowing that the timber merchant would not invoice us immediately.

That night I came home and Joan said there was a letter on the telephone table. I ignored it, had my tea and at the back of mind worried about my action in sanctioning the expenditure when I had been part of an agreement to stall it. Later that evening, I opened the letter. It was from our neighbours and church members Jim and Jean Black and it contained a cheque for £1,000, which was enough to pay for the wood. Jim and Jean said the gift was to be anonymous; but almost 30 years later, I think it is important to acknowledge that gift. One thousand pounds was, I agree, just a fraction of the final £300k, but it was perhaps the most important of all the gifts. 'The widow's mite', Granny Miller used to say, 'The Lord will provide.' And I believe He did!

It was time to bring back the yellow pine pews from the bonded warehouse. It was also time to look for a new pulpit. We visited redundant churches, even antique shops, and eventually found the perfect pulpit in a church that was about to close. The Rev Andrew Lees warmly welcomed us. If we were taken by Andrew's welcome, the wonderful pulpit and Burmese teak pews equally took us. It was a done deal. We would take the lot. Andrew Lees and the good people of Gourock Ashton would be grateful if we could make good use of their pulpit and pews, and we did. The cost for the lot – zero! The cost for the transportation from Gourock to Bonhill...again given generously for nothing by Eric Somerville and his team.

Stained glass windows were removed and replaced in the new sanctuary. Wood and decorative ironwork from the former Bonhill South Church was cleverly incorporated into the new vestibule and porch by Eddie McMurray and his sons Harry and Eric. The first-year pupils from Vale of Leven Academy designed stained glass windows for the porch with the help of artist Lesley McFie. A competition decided the winner and it was agreed Lesley would make the window and that it would be installed at a cost of £400. After the installation of the one window, which we could afford, I was conducting a wedding in the new sanctuary and encouraged those present to have a look at the stained glass. I added that when we had the money we would install another four and that the designs were to hand. As the wedding guests left, one said, 'Ian, install the other four.'

I said, 'Andy, they are £400 a piece!'

He said, 'Install them. Your cheque for £1,600 will be in the post.' As he left he said, 'Ian, not a word. This is between you and me.'

I kept my word and did not mention it until the day I conducted the funeral of Andy Thompson of William Thompson and Sons of Dumbarton. I kept my word and he kept his. Two thousand pounds arrived two days later and so did another five windows designed by Margaret Ann Cairns, Donna Mellis, Fiona Heron, Hannah Collings and Gavin Whitehall. They were installed with their names proudly displayed.

I shared many happy days with the Thompson family - the wedding of Andy and Isa's daughter Sandra to Ernie Colquhoun – but also less happy times - visits to Isa when Andy passed away and the sad occasion when Isa died, followed not long after by their beloved daughter Sandra's passing.

So many local congregations helped our effort. Local businesses and Highdykes School donated a lectern lovingly carved by our senior elder,

Tom Kinloch. There was also a beautiful lectern bible donated by Bonhill School. Local band The Executives staged a concert for us. Margaret Pittam and Morag Kennedy set up a separate fund to raise money - perhaps in ways the Kirk may not have approved of - but it all rolled in.

£100k seemed beyond us. £300k would have been unthinkable, but that is what it eventually cost and as we ended the project we had no debt.

Sadly, our beadle, Davie Kilpatrick, died shortly after the end of the project. His was one of the hardest funerals I have ever taken. I remember before the service just praying, 'Lord, get me through this because I can't do it on my own.'

Not long after, Arthur Menzies was to follow him, but not before leaving me with some lovely memories. One Sunday morning, 30 minutes before the start of the service, I entered the church via the vestry door and strode through the sanctuary towards the adjoining church hall. I had in my hands two large bales of toilet rolls. There was one member of the congregation sitting in the pews at the time. Seeing me coming through she said to Arthur, 'Why does he march through the church with these things?'

Arthur just retorted, 'They are for charity.'

'What do you mean,' asked the member.

'They are for children in need,' he replied.

Arthur died on holiday in Tenerife. The family indicated they would love if his ashes could be interred in the churchyard. They realised the graveyard was no longer in use but still they had hopes. What would be involved? I took an executive decision. Yes, we would do it and no one needed to know. Illegal, but I hope the statute of limitations will save me. I decided we would inter Arthur's ashes beside 'his church'.

We met one Sunday afternoon, just the immediate family and me. I had dug a small hole in advance in order to accommodate the ashes. When the family arrived, they handed me the 'small casket'. Small it was, but larger than I had expected. I knew it would not fit. At that moment rain began to fall. I ushered the family inside and suggested we should wait until the shower was over. I then grabbed a shovel and dashed back out to the 'hole'. Sweat lashing off me, I widened and deepened it while all of the time hearing Arthur's voice: 'No-one should ever trust you with any practical task. In the pulpit you are okay, but that's your limit.' Minutes later, we laid Arthur to rest. Willie Murray succeeded Arthur as Property Convenor. If anything, Willie's opinion of my practical skills was even lower than Arthur's. An opinion that on many an occasion has been completely justified.

*

The Presbytery of Dumbarton met in the old church hall and, at the appointed time, made their way through the churchyard and into the church to give thanks for the completion of the huge rebuilding task. I gave thanks for the dedication of those within the church who supported the effort and the generosity of the many who made it possible.

It was a great day at the end of October 1989 when our exile in Ladyton ended and we returned to our church. I mounted the pulpit to speak to a packed congregation and to welcome new members. It was with a deep sense of pride that one of them was Derek Ian David Miller.

In some ways, this was the beginning of what we hoped to do and be as a congregation. We were back in our building but unless in some way we reached out to the community the exercise would have been a waste of time.

One of the first decisions we took was that our new suite of halls should be opened to all. That decision was soon to be implemented, with Mother and Toddler groups, Play groups and Nurseries meeting during the day. On an occasional basis, tenants' groups and pensioners' groups would also use it. Evening usage was taken up by youth organisations, choir practices, a drama group, Alcoholics Anonymous, study groups and the inevitable church meetings.

Many years before I had been invited to do a series of *Late Call* on STV. That was when the national grid had difficulty coping with those who took *Late Call* as the signal to make a final cup of tea or coffee. I took up the challenge and hopefully acquitted myself reasonably well. I was asked to do probably around eight or nine series until someone else came on the scene. His name was the Rev I.M Jolly. In the face of such competition, I gave up.

Someone must have remembered me, as in the early '90s we were invited to record around 15 individual services for transmission on Sunday mornings. I decided to involve members of the congregation in each service; and how well they acquitted themselves, taking the prayers and readings. I often wondered who watched and was amazed at the letters and messages that came to us from all around the country, almost all of them saying that the congregational singing of the well-known hymns was the highlight.

During this period, I was also invited to supervise of a number of students; then, later, to supervise three young people who had completed their university studies. They were required to do a 'probationary period' before taking up their own church. Each brought something special to our congregation.

Michael Lyall was a son of the manse, a married man who left his full-time employment with the electricity board to undertake studies at Glasgow University. He came to us for the 'finishing touches'. He had great ability with children - with three of his own he had plenty of experience. In due course Michael went to his first charge in Keith and a busload from Bonhill went up to his induction.

Next came Ann Paton, a local lass who had been a schoolteacher before deciding she would become a minister. I always said to each probationer that they would learn from me the things *not* to do. I was open and honest with them, hoping that as they watched me, and evaluated what I did and how I did it, they would make up their own minds as to the pattern their ministries would take. Ann would often chide me for, as she put it, 'flying by the seat of my pants'.

After being there for a few months, I had a short holiday, leaving Ann in control. During that time there was a fearful motor-vehicle accident, with the loss of a young father. She had to conduct the funeral. There was also a multiple drowning in the River Leven (the dangers of which I have already outlined) and then the sad suicide of a lovely young woman who was well known in the community. Ann handled all of those situations. On my return the husband of that young woman said, 'We were devastated when we learned you were on holiday,' but then added, 'no disrespect to you, Ian, but you could not have handled it any better.'

When she recalled her involvement in some difficult pastoral situations to her fellow probationers, they would sympathise and commiserate that she had such an unfeeling boss who would burden her so. Her reply was always, 'Ian would never ask me to do anything he would not be prepared to do himself.' Such was my confidence in Ann that when my own father died she conducted the funeral. If Ann learned from me, I also learned from her.

While she was with us, the church kitchen was being changed. Willie Murray, our property convenor, was pursuing this exercise with vigour but, according to some, not engaging sufficiently with the ladies of the congregation. Some of them complained to Ann. They probably did not mention it to me as Willie was my pal and golf tutor. Ann did. She raised the issue in the church office. She was seated and I was standing against the office radiator. 'Why could they not have spoken to me?' I exploded. There was a long pause and then she said, 'Look at yourself - there is your answer.' Goal to Ann!

Another wee incident amused me. I asked Ann to visit a parishioner who was a dear soul and a 'rerr blether'. Ann was not long in the house when the woman said to her, 'What do you think, the minister's son (our Andrew) is going out with a Catholic girl and I hear it is quite serious. What do you think of that?' Ann answered, 'What would you think if the minister was married to a Catholic?' (Ann's husband, Tom, was a very devout Catholic and totally supportive of Ann's ministry). The woman was stunned but quickly replied, 'Aye hen, but is he good tae ye?' At the end of the day, that was what mattered.

The woman in question was always a joy to visit, without a trace of malice, but the great West of Scotland divide was never far from folks' conscious or unconscious thoughts. Sectarianism appals me and I would like to think I have made some little contribution to lessening its influence in the Vale.

Cameron Langlands was the last in the line of trainee ministers who came to us. He was young and handsome and he fell in love with Bonhill and it with him. He had a most wonderful ability to dramatise the bible stories, with some real purple patches as he vividly brought to life the stories of Jesus and 'the boys' - his description of the disciples. Cameron was involved with our drama group and proved himself an able thespian. He too was great with children. It was no surprise that at the end of his time with us he was called to the neighbouring vacant parish of Renton. Sadly, after a few years Cameron felt called to hospital chaplaincy. I have always felt he was a huge loss to the parish ministry.

Near the end of my ministry, we invited Cameron back to preach in Bonhill. It was a very emotional moment for Bonhill and Cameron. At the end of his sermon, in a wonderfully loving and spontaneous act, the Bonhill congregation rose and applauded. You might say there was not a dry eye in the house! Mind you, a month or so later, Ann Paton also preached as an invited guest. Of course, I was able to tell her that when Cameron had preached the congregation had risen to their feet and applauded. I told her it was not liable to happen again, but of course it did - they rose for Ann as well.

It was the 30th June, 2012, when I bade the congregation farewell, before they did the same for me!

CHAPTER SIX

HOSPITALS AND COMMUNITY

IF I were to be asked what should be available freely to every member of our community my answer would be simple: health and education.

My involvement with schools started in 1975 and, 40 years later, I still appreciate the privilege of being involved with the young people in whose hands lie the hopes of our community.

The head teacher at Bonhill Primary was the redoubtable Margaret Henderson. She was of the old school and was in charge of the ship. I made contact with her upon my arrival, was made most welcome, and became part of their weekly assemblies.

It was late in 1975 and the school was in the grip of Christmas excitement. They were to stage a nativity play in the church. It would run for a few nights in order to let all the parents and grandparents of the 400-plus children see the event. I sat and watched, entranced by the performance. It seemed to outdo Oberammergau's famous Passion Play. Angels with glittering wings were strategically placed on the stairs that led up to each side of the pulpit. Gabriel had pride of place in the pulpit, standing on a chair to give appropriate elevation. Mrs Henderson pulled the strings, encouraging and exhorting her charges like a Broadway producer. The result was amazing. The applause was rapturous.

The following morning, I hotfooted it to the school, prepared to be lavish in my appreciation of the production. As I entered the door, Mrs H was in full flight. The target of her verbal assault stood silently, taking it all in and looking at her with the most amazing big brown eyes. My initial reaction was to turn and run. Two things stopped me. The child turned and looked at me with pleading eyes. Mrs Henderson addressed me. 'Mr Miller, Tony was talking to the angels in your church last night. What do you have to say to him?'

Facetiously, I might have answered, 'No better place to talk to angels,' but such a flippant response would not have been appreciated. Instead I muttered something along the lines of, 'Tony that was not very nice.' Mrs H did not appreciate this inept response and I was banished to the school office.

I was later to discover the story behind the incident. It appeared Tony had been seated in the gallery of the church, which was a mere few yards from the pulpit steps, and during the performance he was arranging an assignation with one of the angels. Therefore, he was indeed 'talking to the angels'!

Tony must have detected sympathy in my response, for he was to repay me a few days later by telling me the names of some people who had helped themselves to items from my garage. I still see Tony from time to time. I have never forgotten that incident and I suspect he hasn't either.

At that time, the school was full and overflowing. Many of the pupils were in temporary accommodation in the playground. The local authority decided Bonhill needed another school and so Highdykes was built in the late '70s, right at the top of the hill, almost above the snow line, but with a marvellous view of the Clyde and the Loch. Mrs Henderson was appointed the first head teacher and she took me with her as chaplain. I also continued at Bonhill and was delighted when Elizabeth Chirrey (Margaret's deputy) was appointed head teacher.

In some ways Elizabeth was not dissimilar to Margaret in the sense that she was 'in control', but she also had a wonderful sense of humour and warmth. She continued my weekly visits and our 'after service' chats over coffee were great therapy for me. Elizabeth became both my friend and confidante.

I am quite convinced that drama classes must form part of a teacher's training. I witnessed the perfect example. Elizabeth was in the act of pouring coffee when there was a timid knock on the door. She excused herself and opened the door and an exchange took place. I only heard Elizabeth's side of it, which went as follows.

'Yes... You what? I do not believe it. I have never heard such a thing from a Primary One boy. I am shocked and may I say that the Rev Miller, who is sitting with me, would be quite appalled by what I am hearing. Can I be assured there will be no repetition? Can I also presume that you are very sorry? Well I am glad to hear that. Now get back to your class.'

I waited to hear the story. Instead, Elizabeth with her usual sweet smile said, 'You don't take sugar, Ian, do you?' End of story. It was at that point that I realised teachers are also consummate actors.

Shortly afterwards I was invited to act as chaplain at Bonhill's third primary school, Ladyton. All of the schools were different, as were the head teachers. Ladyton's Jean McLuskie was a character with theatrical connections. Her cousin was Jimmy Logan. I could see the likeness. Margaret and Elizabeth were involved in their local churches but Jean, even though she had no such connection, was enthusiastic to have me involved. She was clever and innovative and very much her own woman, with a commendable attitude towards authority. She and I had a very warm and easy relationship. She took an interest in what I would do with the children. Sometimes she would encourage me not to wind the kids up, but just prior to one assembly she asked me what I was going to talk about. She had not done this before and I tried as best as I could to outline my talk.

'What has that to do with your shoes?' she asked.

'Absolutely nothing,' I replied.

'Then why,' said she 'do you have one brown and one black shoe on?'

There was no answer. I dashed out of her office without another word and drove home like a banshee to rectify the error.

Nativity plays were always a source of joy, but also mishaps, and this added to the experience. One Christmas, at Ladyton, Mary number one took ill on the morning of the performance, Mary number two took cold feet and refused to perform and Mary number three was plucked from obscurity. I vividly remember her stately progress down the aisle on top of a wooden donkey. I was mesmerised. The donkey seemed to be moving of its own accord. Then I noticed, in the corner of the stage, the 'Janny' pulling on string. The string had been attached to the front of the donkey and then re-routed through an eyelet on the stage and thence to the invisible off-stage 'Janny'. It was very effective.

I have watched angels picking their noses and shepherds fighting with their crooks like ninja warriors. Whatever the disaster or mishap there has always been an adherence to the old theatrical dictum, 'the show must go on'.

I heard of one pageant in which a young man named Ben was determined to be Joseph but was overlooked for the part. Instead, he was offered the part of the innkeeper. He was determined to refuse but eventually his mother's threat of reduced privileges forced him to reconsider. He was to have his revenge however. When Mary and Joseph appeared at the inn and asked if there was any room, Ben answered, to the great surprise of Mary and Joseph – not to mention the teachers and the assembled audience - 'Yes, no problem, we have plenty of rooms, in you come.' Mary and Joseph were stunned, but Joseph suddenly moved forward as if inspecting the premises and came out with the winning line, 'Oh, I would not live here, this place is a dump, it looks like a cowshed.'

It always pays to keep things simple whenever you are working with children. In all things, there is always the temptation to be that little more adventurous. A very prestigious church in America gave in to that temptation, with dramatic consequences. They brought in a real live donkey for their nativity. Mary looked quite regal as she sat side-saddle, smiling enigmatically as she progressed down the long aisle. Donkeys are unpredictable creatures and this one, true to its character, just stopped and stubbornly refused to move. Office-bearers moved in; they pushed and shoved with no result. At that moment, the organist decided to get in on the act and switch the focus from the unexpected drama. Pulling out every stop of the huge pipe organ, he played the crashing opening note of Bach's Toccata and Fugue. This produced a result. The donkey got a fright, which had a gastrointestinal effect. Shovels and air fresheners were needed to restore some degree of normality. Pregnant or not, Mary shot off the donkey, leaving it and the ordure behind her, before walking regally up the aisle onto the chancel as if nothing had happened. A true professional.

Communicating with children and engaging with them has been a privilege. It has also been a challenge. When speaking to them I have tended to be quite animated. At one end-of-term service in the church, I was moving around the chancel area like a teenager when I found that my foot, instead of being on the step, was in mid-air. I went down as quickly as if I had been felled by a Muhammad Ali uppercut. However, I bounded back up as though nothing had happened. I did notice that the faces of the teachers had gone a little white. One child raised his hand. I should have ignored it but did not. 'What do you want to ask?' I said. He said, 'Mr Miller, you were just like a penguin!'

I was not going to enquire as to this similarity between me and the penguin and so continued with my talk. At the end of the service, however, I did enquire of him as to his perception that the penguin and I might have something in common and so he explained. Apparently he was a devotee of nature programs and he simply said, 'You see when the penguins are being chased by the Orca killer whales? They come out of the water like a torpedo and land on the ice flow. And that's just what you did.'

I did not take the conversation any further. Mind you, as the older children appeared for the second service, they were very quick to ask me if there would be an encore!

When Margaret Henderson retired at Highdykes, Rena Murray took her place and then she was succeeded by her second-in-command Irene Robertson. It was always a joy to visit the school and my visits to the staff room made me realise what a happy school these two women had created. Rena and Irene were a wonderful partnership and had one thing very definitely in common. They were great 'greeters'. The end of term service, with the P7s going on to High School, was always a big, emotional event, with Rena and Irene finishing a box of Kleenex between them. I suppose at times like that, it did help to have a chaplain.

From the late '70s onward I became involved with the Vale of Leven Academy - VOLA. I found all of the head teachers welcomed my involvement, from Tom Murray to Duncan Penny, Neil McKinnon, Terry Lanagan, Gus McDonald and Catriona Robertson. To speak to a packed assembly hall was special. I heard some scary stories from some of my colleagues – tales of disruption - but never once did I experience that at VOLA.

Duncan Penny's tenure coincided with my sons' time at the school and accordingly I saw more of Duncan. He was a character, a man's man, an athlete. He had the great ability to call a spade a spade, and that was on a good day. Terry Lanagan, who later became director of education, had a wonderful ability to get alongside the pupils.

Davie Calder and the late Dougie Morrison, along with a few others, had an enormous influence on Derek and Andrew. Their encouragement and support helped them to become the people they are today.

Davie Calder was a character, probably even to some degree a maverick, yet the pupils loved him. End of term before the summer holidays often featured a curry cooked by Dave on the chemistry department's Bunsen burners. Sadly, Dave left this world suddenly and unexpectedly. He had taken early retirement and although he did some supply work, I think he missed his day-to-day contact with the pupils. I conducted his funeral. He had left explicit instructions that I should do so. The actual cause of his death was unascertained. There was nothing suspicious, but at that time, just after 'Shipman', medical examiners were reluctant to add their signatures to crematorium forms when the cause was not certain. Cardross, our local crematorium, refused to sign the forms, but Clydebank agreed. Then with details of the service now in the public domain, the decision was reversed.

Davie was unique in life; and in death, that sense of uniqueness remained. It is the only service I have conducted where the deceased has been brought into the service room but, instead of the curtains closing, has gone back out of the crematorium to a standing ovation. I suspect that in his repose he would have had a quiet smile on his face.

The following day there was a quiet cremation service with the family at Craigton Crematorium in Glasgow. Though the situation has been explained to me, and I understand that it relates to the views taken by the different medical referees, I am left feeling that this lack of uniformity often causes additional distress to grieving families.

*

My other community passion has been healthcare. In the early '80s, I was appointed part-time chaplain at Vale of Leven Hospital. I held this post for almost 30 years and, during that time, my respect and admiration for the committed and faithful staff never diminished. At that time, the hospital was a fully functioning District General Hospital serving an area that stretched from Dumbarton to the far-flung parts of Argyll. It offered a 24/7 accident and emergency department, emergency and elective surgery, acute medical care and a full range of maternity and gynaecological services. A small percentage of patients who needed specialised or sub-specialised care were transferred to the larger Glasgow hospitals. Most mental health cases were transferred either to Lochgilphead or to Gartnavel Royal until our MP, John McFall, opened the Christie Ward. Most of our healthcare needs were met locally, but things were to change.

The Conservative government of the time was determined to devolve management to a more local level. Accordingly, the Lomond Integrated Healthcare Trust was set up. Its responsibility would be to manage and monitor the Vale hospital but also the care provided in the local community. Under the new proposals the Board would comprise of an independent chairman, a chief executive, heads of accounts, human resources and estates, and of course representation from the medical staff. There would also be a number of non-executive appointments.

These would be people with either some sort of talent in terms of finance, business, law or the community. It was widely believed that they would be 'Tory placemen or placewomen' as the Secretary of State for Scotland, who at that time was Michael Forsyth, would appoint them. Names of the appointments were released. All respectable and decent people with good pedigrees. In the eyes of the local MP, there was the omission of anyone who was directly in touch with staff and the community of the Vale of Leven, where the hospital was a major employer. He decided that the hospital chaplain might fit the bill. Forsyth took some convincing but John, later to become Lord Alcluith, was a powerful persuader. I do not think Michael stood a chance and he bowed to John's demands. Therefore, I became for the first and probably only time in my life 'a Tory placeman'. In fairness, I can safely say that none of the non-execs turned out to be placemen or placewomen.

By this time the Trust was up and running, so it was only to be expected that this late addition was viewed with some degree of suspicion. As I sat for the first time in the boardroom, I got the feeling that my appointment was not universally welcomed. The chairman, Steven Newell, did make the point that it was nice to have a representative from the faith community who was actively involved in the hospital, but the medical director, Eric Taylor, a man of powerful intellect and, I was to discover later, a quite wicked sense of humour, asked if there might be invites to other faith communities. At that moment, I felt silence was the best option.

I must confess, however, that was the first and only time I did not feel welcome and valued. Eric became a friend and I admired his debating skills and his humanity, which he was quite good at hiding - after all, he was a surgeon. He was also a man with prophetic foresight and saw the direction that surgery and acute medical care was taking. I disagreed with him then but now admit he called it perfectly. He warned us of what was ahead but we failed to heed his warning. In some ways, my time spent at Lomond Health Care was among the best of an almost

Proud parents with our first child.

Ian and Joan having even more good times

Bonhill Kirk Session prior to the renovation project in the early eighties.

Get me to the church on time! The only way when Oasis are in town...

15-year experience with the health trusts and boards in all their different guises. My non-executive director colleagues were people of integrity, every single one of them bringing something of worth to what we were trying to do. David Morell, Eileen Gorrie, the late Archie McKenzie, Liz McHard and later Marion Marchbanks. The executive team was an interesting bunch, but two in particular I would have trusted with my life - David Watson and Ron Arbuckle.

Being a small hospital and a tight community, the staff were always able to keep us abreast of possible developments and changes and advise of their concerns. They often persuaded me at least, that staff saw changes, which were in my opinion negative, as positive.

John Kelly was a prince of a man and his services to nursing were recognised by the award of an MBE. John was a gentleman, a devout Catholic, a committed Christian and a realist. He always had time for me if I was agonising over any possible board decision. He was not alone. Lifelong friend, and former babysitter, Shiona McKay in midwifery, and Liz Hunter and others in general nursing were all great resources. John McFall MP and then, at a later stage, Jackie Baillie our MSP were fiercely supportive and committed to the retention of local services.

Later the acute services at Vale of Leven Hospital were transferred to the Argyll and Clyde Health Board Acute Trust and the community healthcare services north of the Clyde placed in a Primary Care Trust chaired by Vivian Dance, a local businessperson from Helensburgh. I was seconded onto the Acute Trust with its headquarters in Paisley. In many ways the changes Eric Taylor predicted began to happen, steady bacon-slicing of existing services. Eric predicted the first service to go would be the Special Care Baby Unit (SCBU), then Obs and Gyn, then Anaesthetics, A&E, then consultant-led Maternity, then Emergency Surgery, to be followed by Acute Medical Care. I may have got the order wrong but more or less that is what happened. I reckon I opposed all of the changes and still feel there are services that could and should be provided at the Vale.

There was one board decision that was to come back to haunt us. Cost-cutting was always on the agenda. It seemed bureaucracy in the Health Service was growing exponentially and empires were expanding, so something had to go. It was suggested we cut cleaning schedules. The non-execs, without exception, voiced their concerns. In particular, Archie McKenzie, formerly a police officer of high rank and at that time Depute Lord Lieutenant, was particularly strident in his opposition. Archie's argument was that to reduce the cleaning regime would run the risk of increasing infection. Eventually the senior nurse, in an almost patronising way, said, 'But Archie, sometimes hospitals can be too clean.' Archie was a big man and often big men seem to acquire a special mildness. At 6ft 6ins, no one was likely to be a threat to Archie, but at that moment all his mildness disappeared. He flared up like a Roman candle. One of the more printable things he said was, 'One day we will regret this decision.'

In 2007/8, there was an outbreak of Clostridium Difficile - C Diff - in the hospital. Sadly there were a number of deaths. Most of the patients who died were frail or elderly, with underlying health problems, but their demise was hastened by the bacterium.

There was an outcry. Fingers were pointed in various directions, and calls made for a full public inquiry. At that moment, I thought of Archie's prediction! I know the staff at the coalface felt deeply about it. I had seen evidence of a deteriorating standard of cleanliness and the staff were aware of this. I know they had complained and morale was low. It has always been my conviction that, whether the issue is health, education, local authority, Church or almost any other enterprise, those at the top of the tree have the skill, ability and ingenuity to apportion the blame further down that tree. The staff certainly felt they were hung out to dry, though in due course the public inquiry did indicate some very definite Health Board shortcomings.

My time on the Argyll and Clyde Health Board was challenging and the drift of services from the Vale Hospital was gathering momentum. Local interests were well served by Councillors Jim Flynn, Ian

Robertson, Billy Petrie and myself. On one occasion Jim, Billy and I were carpeted by the then chairperson, John Mullan, who accused us of leaking something to the press. It felt like being in the headmaster's office the way we were addressed and accused. At all times the non-executive directors and local authority representatives did try to do their best for the NHS and their local community.

It became obvious that the Argyll and Clyde Health Board were facing financial difficulties and the Scottish Government took the decision to dissolve it. All services became the remit of Greater Glasgow and Clyde Health Board. I was prevailed upon by Bill Clark, the Director of Social Work at West Dunbartonshire, to put myself forward for consideration. Jackie Baillie also encouraged my interest.

After meeting with Sir John Arbuthnot, the chair of the Health Board, I realised I was wasting my time. He asked me what talents and experience I would bring to the Board. Did I have accountancy knowledge? Legal knowledge? Business expertise? To all of these questions I had to answer in the negative. I eventually said, 'I bring knowledge of my community and, I hope, good interpersonal skills.' When he said, 'I trust you do not think you will be campaigning for your local hospital,' or words to that effect, I realized, with some relief, that it was probably time to kiss goodbye to Health Board politics. Thankfully, Sir John Arbuthnot was replaced by Andrew Robertson, in my opinion a much more human and engaging individual.

In fairness to Greater Glasgow and Clyde Health Board, they had just completed a strategic review as to how and where their acute services would be delivered. The last thing they needed was to have the entire Argyll and Clyde area thrust upon them. I suspect that when they engaged with our community they were very reluctant to bin their plan and start again, so I believe we were shoe-horned into their existing plan. It is the only logical explanation I can come up with to explain why it was decided that our acute care would be delivered at the Royal Alexandria Hospital in Paisley. A bitter and strident campaign was mounted in an attempt to ensure that our acute care would be delivered north of the River Clyde, pointing out that the Erskine Bridge was indeed 'a bridge too far'. The only way Paisley could reasonably be reached was by car. Public transport involved at least two train journeys and one bus journey and then a long walk to the RAH, which was inconveniently set on a hill.

In the minds of our community there was a unanimous view that Paisley was wrong for us. That view remains. Many a patient will indicate it is the last place they want to be taken in the event of sudden illness, but we have no choice. This is not to denigrate the quality of care that is delivered there.

Thankfully, there is hope that things may change. Jackie Baillie MSP has fronted a campaign to have the Royal Jubilee hospital extended to serve us with A&E, acute medical and surgical care and to have as many services as possible retained at the Vale.

I have met with a number of Health Ministers, including Lord James Hamilton, Sam Galbraith, Susan Deacon, Andy Kerr, Nicola Sturgeon and Alex Neil. There were signs from Nicola and especially Alex that our pleas were being listened to. The Health Board, in the persons of Andrew Robertson and Robert Calderwood, also gave an indication that they would be prepared to include some of our suggestions in their option appraisal. Sadly, Shona Robison looks as if she is not prepared to pursue this option. What behind the scenes deal caused this change, I doubt we will ever know. A leaked Health Board document in January 2016 makes clear that there is a threat of a further reduction in services. In the opinion of many people in the Vale, the very existence of the hospital is under threat. This means the fight for the retention of services and the return of others will intensify. Throughout it all, my affection and support for the staff at the Vale of Leven Hospital is undiminished. Over the years, as a community, we have owed a debt to the surgeons, clinicians, nurses, auxiliaries and ancillary staff who have served us so well.

As the hospital chaplain, I became a confidante to many of the staff. I also had a great working arrangement with my Catholic colleague,

Father Brendan Murtagh. Brendan was greatly loved by the staff. He was often invited to their nights out, an honour they never conferred on me!

We both took advantage of an opportunity to demonstrate our togetherness. The Alexander Brothers offered to do a TV show in the church at Bonhill. It was decided that Brendan and I would co-host it. At the end of the day, Brendan decided to opt out of the limelight and asked John Corcoran, a member of St Mary's RC Church, to co-host with me. It was a great night and STV captured it all for the nation. The programme was entitled *See You On Sunday* and so the show ended with me saying to the packed audience, 'Thanks for coming and see you on Sunday.' Many did not take up the offer!

Schools and hospitals were big in my ministry. It was with great sadness that I witnessed an arson attack on the Vale Academy, which largely destroyed a considerable part of the main building. The then head teacher, Terry Lanagan, was of course called out in the early hours of the morning and he stood witnessing the conflagration and the efforts of the fire service to limit the damage. As he watched, a young man sidled up beside him and said, 'Mr Lanagan, I hope they get the b****** that did this.' Well they did, and it turned out to be that same young man.

For quite a few years, the pupils were housed in temporary accommodation as the local authority searched for a permanent solution. Eventually it was decided that a new Vale Academy should be built and on the same campus and a new primary school erected to accommodate the pupils of Bonhill and Renton. This proposal was not well received. It would have involved a considerable journey for the primary pupils from the far reaches of Bonhill, down across the River Leven to the new Vale site. Parents also expressed concern that siting a large secondary school and a primary school on the same site was not advisable. At a fiery meeting in a packed Bonhill Church, the community voiced their opposition.

West Dunbartonshire Council had a rethink and decided to abandon the joint campus plan. The new school was built directly across from the old Bonhill Primary School. I count it a great honour to have been asked to open it officially. My name is on the plaque. Sadly, the old Bonhill Primary School was also subsequently burned down in an act of vandalism.

On retirement, I thought my school days were finally over. I would have missed that greatly. However, Highdykes and Ladyton asked if I would continue as chaplain and I am involved in Christie Park, a few hundred yards from home.

Many years ago, the Vale of Leven supplied many singers to the famous Orpheus Choir. To hear children of Christie Park School sing with such enthusiasm and musicality indicates that the Vale of Leven is still a valley of song.

With school roll numbers dropping it was decided that there had to be some degree of rationalisation of school buildings. Ladyton and Highdykes schools have come together in the extensively refurbished former St Ronan's building. Meanwhile, the pupils of St Ronan's have moved into the former Ladyton School and the site of Highdykes will now, in all probability, be developed for housing. The way the staff and pupils of Ladyton and Highdykes came together to plan for this event impressed me. I was delighted to be involved with staff and pupils.

A new name and a new school uniform were important issues for the combined Ladyton and Highdykes school and our comments were noted by the local authority. I was even more delighted that one child thought it might be called the Rev Ian Miller School. All the names were put to a vote. The Rev Ian Miller got no votes - even I did not vote for it. I was delighted, however, that my own personal preference - Lennox Primary School - was chosen. After all, the old historic name for the area was 'the lands of Lennox'.

Another chapter in the life of schooling in the Vale is now being written.

CHAPTER SEVEN

WEDDINGS

LIVING near Loch Lomond, I suppose it was natural I would do more than my fair share of weddings, especially when coupled with the expectation of the congregation that I should turn no one away. What a privilege it was to be part of so many couples' big days, hopefully one of the happiest of their lives. It also brought me into contact with a variety of folk, some of whom have become friends; others simply became briefly a part of my life, and I of theirs. They also provided a host of interesting, sometimes amusing stories, for no two weddings are ever the same.

Every wedding should have its share of both laughter and tears. Grooms especially would stumble over the words, particularly the word 'covenant', which I often used. For example, 'I promise and covenant to be a loving, faithful and loyal husband to you.' One young man attempted the word three times and then eventually, with despair on his face, said, 'Och whatever it is ah'll dae it anyway.' I suppose that is the kind of man most girls are looking for. *Covenant* means a bargain and, in my experience, most men got a good bargain. Another lad at the same juncture in the service said, 'I promise to dae that wurd that you just said.' I hope he did.

It is a big day and most participants are nervous. One young man in Luss Church hoped the ground would open up. Instead of taking his lawful wedded wife, his mind had drifted beyond the ceremony to later on that night. A Freudian slip stunned the congregation when he described her as his 'lawful bedded wife.' His face turned 50 shades of grey. Another young man promised to be 'loyal faithful and lustful.' In both instances, they were never to live it down.

One of the most exotic of all weddings took place on the shores of the Indian Ocean. Initially it was borne out of tragedy for Willie McDonald, the man behind the Antartex empire. He had asked if I would be willing to conduct the wedding of his beautiful daughter, Anna, to her Kenyan sweetheart Lengai, at the little country church of Kilmaronock. I readily agreed. Willie was a lovely man, a true gentleman who was held in the highest regard by all who worked for him. Sadly, with the dates of the nuptials set, Willie died unexpectedly while on a visit to London with the love of his life Malla.

After some time, Anna decided it would be too emotional for her and Lengai to be married at Kilmaronock and changed the venue to Kenya. Would I be willing to travel? What an opportunity! It was an unforgettable experience. We stayed at the Hemingways Resort for a week, a haunt of the rich and famous near Malindi, with only the beach between us and the surging waters of the Indian Ocean.

Interestingly, at Nairobi airport, Joan and I were sitting together, wondering which of the people waiting for the shuttle to Malindi might also be wedding guests, when from behind us a gruff Scots voice said, 'Where's Stan Jones? You two are always joined at the hip.' Stan was a golfing pal of mine and was one of the Vale's characters. I turned around and there was Robert Gray, a resident of Gartocharn, who, along with his wife Mary, and Martin and Freyda Wedgewood, were also attending the wedding. Freyda was a natural organiser and the rest of us just went along with her as she placed us appropriately at the hotel dining table, man - woman, man - woman and so on. Joan was never into this and came close to rebellion. For some unaccountable reason she did as she was told as, I suspect, did Martin. They were great company.

Every country has its idiosyncrasies and Kenya was no exception. This five-star hotel had the most primitive urinal, which can best be described as a stainless steel trough. At the bottom of this trough, running the length of the wall, was a series of long poles of ice about four inches thick. I have still to determine their purpose. Probably it was to reduce the effect of any offensive odours. After a few Kenyan beers,

Robert and I used to retire to the said urinal, telling the women, 'We are away to break the ice.' They never knew what we were talking about.

The wedding day arrived and what an event it was. I can still see Anna, flaxen-haired and blue-eyed, wedding dress billowing behind her, being escorted by her brother, along the sand, barefoot and radiant, towards her handsome groom. He was dressed in what I can only presume was the sort of costume that white Kenyans wear. We even attempted a few hymns 'a cappella', our singing not quite drowned out by sound of the waves on the shore.

The reception was held under the stars. It was warm, atmospheric and wonderful. We had a few days to recover at Hemingways, which included a visit to Anna and Lengai's house. The property was staggeringly innovative; it even had a tree growing through it and wonderful meandering verandas. It gave a new meaning to 'tree house'.

It was our intention to board the little plane at Malindi and return to Nairobi, where Joan and I hoped to join a safari. However, the journey home was not without incident. Arriving at the airport, there was some police activity. We waited. Others seemed to be boarding the small prop-plane back to Nairobi. Then some official-looking people with briefcases told us that the plane was full. However, we were booked. We showed the airport staff our tickets, even our reserved seats, but all to no avail. The flight was full. We were due to start our safari the next day.

The Kenyan Airways staff eventually said they could arrange a taxi to Mombasa where we might be able to catch a flight to Nairobi. They would try to hold up the Mombasa flight but could not promise. With everything being uncertain, we decided to take the risk. Andrew and Mia Wilson, who were wedding guests, and we Millers poured ourselves into an ancient taxi and took off. 'Took off' was an apt description, with the driver avoiding potholes that would rival the craters on the Moon. The livestock and wildlife seemed to think the road was theirs. We passed shanty towns, in stark contrast to the luxury we had just enjoyed at Hemingways. We watched smiling-faced youngsters returning from school. It was an eventful and sometimes scary journey. The four of us did not talk much. We spent most of our time hanging onto our seats and glancing at our watches hoping we would make Mombasa in time.

There was one lovely little snippet of conversation. Andrew Wilson (he is in fact a titled person) said, 'How do you think we would have fared if Freyda had been with us?' I answered that we would probably have got on the flight from Malindi. 'You are probably right,' he said. 'Either that or we would be in the jail.'

We did make the Nairobi flight, which, thankfully had been held up by a technical issue. At least that was the story. Joan and I stayed at the famous Stanley Hotel. In the past, in the pre-internet days, it was a great meeting place for travellers hoping to meet up with friends. In the main coffee area there was a gigantic tree growing up through the building. People would write messages and stick them on the trunk. For example, 'Mary, meet you at the Nairobi Saracen Heid on Wednesday - Jimmy from Glasgow.' Or something like that. Probably a forerunner of Facebook.

The following day Joan and I set off on our safari to the Masai Mara. We travelled through the Great Rift Valley, stopping at places of interest. Our overnight stops were an experience. We heard lions roaring, hippopotami rampaging up river beds, the chattering of monkeys...every conceivable jungle noise. It was very exciting but never unnerving. We would sit in the evening, quite entranced, overlooking a small river as crocodiles emerged from the murky waters and slowly crept up the banks to devour whatever scraps the hotel had left out.

The staff would provide the crocs with their evening meal; but, before the crocs emerged, vultures would arrive, pecking, fighting and squabbling while keeping a careful eye on the slow-moving predators as they advanced. Some would even remain as the crocs began their meal, nipping in now and again to grab a tasty morsel before quickly moving out of range of snapping jaws.

I suppose, for me, what was most surprising was the abundance of wildlife. Before going, I had wondered if it would be a sort of upgraded safari park. Or would we know the animals were there but not be able to see them? We saw them all. Lions, warthogs, wildebeest, elephants, leopards, chimpanzees, monkeys, ostriches, crocs, vultures, eagles, hyenas, giraffes, rhinos, hippos, antelope (in all their varieties), cheetahs and so many more. It was a once-in-a-lifetime experience, and Kamanga was a wonderful guide.

He took us to a Masai village, where the residents welcomed us like royalty and took us down to the river to see the hippos. Normally everything we saw was from the safety of Kamanga's four-wheel-drive but suddenly we were out in the open and feeling exposed. We were invited into their homes, which were very dark and had a fly population in the thousands. Mind you, when we discovered what they used as a raw material to create the building blocks, we were not surprised. Cow dung and flies do go together!

The highlight for us was a hot air balloon trip over the Masai Mara, looking down on herds of wildebeest on their annual migration back to the Serengeti. Periodically the fire heater of the hot air balloon would be switched off and we would drift silently along, 1,000 feet above the ground. You could hear the grunts of the wildebeest as they made their long pilgrimage across the plains.

On the last day Kamanga said, 'You are a Reverend. Would you like to come and see our new church?'

I said I would, so Kamanga took us to Kerwa Presbyterian Church on the outskirts of Nairobi. It was just a simple, empty building with a few workers arranging seats.

'When is it opening?' I asked.

'Tomorrow,' was the succinct answer.

It did not look as if it would be ready.

'How many are you expecting?'

'Oh anything up to 4,000.'

I looked around and figured that if the seats were in position it would probably accommodate 500 or so. When I pointed this out to him he just said, 'No problem.'

We were greeted like dignitaries and spent some time with Kamanga and his friends as they prepared for the grand opening.

Suddenly Joan said to them, 'We have about 200 dollars left. We won't need them so please take them for the church.'

The response was immediate: 'We need a keyboard and we will use your gift towards it.' We bid them farewell and the next morning jetted back to the UK.

The following Sunday, I told the congregation of our experiences and, in particular, of the visit to Kerwa Church and its congregation's intention to buy a keyboard. That afternoon a member of the congregation phoned me to say she was moving house and had a nearly-new Yamaha Clavinova. Could I get it to Kenya? Of course I could! I would accept the gift. On replacing the receiver, however, I did wonder how I would get it to Nairobi, but on speaking to Kamanga he did not have a worry. 'The Lord will provide.' I hoped he would.

For the next few weeks, I enquired of various shipping agents and freight carriers to ascertain the cost of getting one Clavinova to Kenya. I received not one quote or reply. Kamanga, who was monitoring my progress, again counselled me not to worry, that the Lord had a plan. I was beginning to fear that the Lord had left me with the heavy end. In desperation, I made a phone call to Allan Galt, of Galt Transport in Dumbarton. 'Allan,' I said. 'I am looking for advice. Can you put me in touch with someone who can help me get a keyboard to Kenya.'

'No problem,' said Allan. 'I will pick it up.'

'But what's the sense of that, Allan?' I said, 'It will simply be lying in your yard instead of my church.'

'I am telling you, I will pick it up. Don't you worry about it.'

'What about cost?' I asked.

'Just you forget it. All you need to know is that I will get it to Kenya.' Moreover, he did.

Kamanga's response? 'I told you the Lord would provide.'
And I suppose he did, via Allan Galt.

*

A year or so after my Kenyan experience, I was invited to Hollywood to conduct a wedding. I told the congregation and was besieged with questions. Which of the grade A celebrities had called upon my services? I remained tight-lipped and just encouraged them to scan the newspapers. Later I had to admit it was the Hollywood that is just outside Bangor, Northern Ireland.

One day I received a phone call from a Jill Setterington. Her enquiry was simple - 'Will you marry me at Loch Lomond Golf Club?'

My answer was simple. 'Did your father ever play for Rangers?'

'Indeed he did,' she said. 'Did you know my Dad?'

'No, I did not' I replied. 'But there is no way I am conducting the marriage of any lass whose father played for RFC.' (I am a die-hard Celtic fan).

There was a long pause and then Jill answered, 'You are at it.'

And indeed, I was.

Dennis Setterington was a very accomplished footballer, who had the misfortune to play at the same time as the legendary Scotland and Rangers player Jim Baxter, otherwise I am sure Dennis would have risen to greater prominence. Jill, a lawyer, was a bonnie extrovert lass who could never get out of the habit of calling me 'Reverend Miller' (and still cannot) even though I have often told her, 'The only folk who call me that are usually looking for money.' In due course, it was my privilege to marry Jill and Ian Livingstone, whose father was David. When introduced, I managed to refrain from adapting the H M Stanley line and so did *not* say, 'Mr Livingstone, I presume?'

At the end of the reception, they presented me with something huge that was covered in gold paper. It looked for all the world as if I had acquired the Mona Lisa. It had the appearance of a very large picture frame. I tore the paper off and there, hooked onto an empty frame, was a football strip in blue - Rangers blue, with the RFC crest and, on the back, *No 1*, and underneath *Rev Ian Miller*.

I was also privileged to conduct the marriage ceremonies for the former Rangers and Scotland manager Walter Smith's sons, Neil and Steven. Neil had the good sense to marry Karen Haggarty, whose grandmother was a staunch supporter of Bonhill Church. Jessie ran The Stewart School of Dancing and had an enormous influence for good on so many young lives in the Vale of Leven. Her legacy lives on - Christie Park School is next door to the dance studio and the present head teacher, Laura Penny, was one of Jessie's protégées. Laura similarly inspires the next generation of the Vale's youngsters.

Steven married into a Celtic-supporting family. He and his best man encouraged me to wear the RFC top supplied by Jill. I did so at the reception, but also wore a green clerical shirt with a dog collar, which I hope in some way resembled a hoop.

During both of the Smith weddings, I had the privilege of sitting beside Walter and Ethel Smith and found then to be engaging company. Walter comes, like most of us, from an ordinary background. His honesty and integrity shines through. He has not lost touch with his roots in Carmyle. Ethel is the perfect foil.

I have conducted the weddings of a few other football players, including Mark Brown. Mark has played for Rangers and Celtic plus both of the Inverness teams, and is now playing with my local team - Dumbarton.

I also married Steven Thomson. Steven's family has strong connections with the Isle of Arran in the Firth of Clyde. Steven spent most summers there when a child. His mother is the godmother of our son, Andrew, and one of our dearest friends. It was a wonderful day. The sun shone on Steven and Joanne. Steven was playing for Rangers at the time and was expecting 'pelters' from me. Especially since Celtic were well ahead in the league as their wedding drew closer. Then Celtic faltered. It all came down to the last games of the season, with Celtic playing Motherwell and Rangers playing Dunfermline.

Rangers ran out easy winners, but Celtic were also winning 1-0 as their match neared its close. Then, catastrophically, Scott McDonald scored for Motherwell. Still, Celtic could win the league with that score. Then McDonald scored another just two minutes later. Game over. The helicopter, which had been hovering to take the league trophy to Celtic, turned and delivered the silverware to the jubilant boys in blue.

That meant that all of the slagging I had prepared for Steven had to go. I was suddenly on silent mode. I did, however, make my own little statement by wearing a small pair of Celtic cufflinks. Not small enough for them to be missed by Barry Ferguson, the then Rangers captain, when he and I were standing at the bar of the Kinloch Hotel in Blackwaterfoot, Arran. He caught hold of me and I have the photo to prove it. Football players often get a bad press for their behaviour and there were a number at Stevie's wedding. They were lovely people, every single one. It was just that they played for the wrong team!

I conducted the marriage of the former Celtic player Darren O'Dea and his delightful bride, Mellissa Cheung, at Bonhill Church in a wonderful ceremony, complete with a gospel choir that threatened to raise the roof. Shortly afterwards I married Rangers' Kenny Miller; then Charlie Adams, who is now with Stoke City.

One I missed was that great Liverpool goalkeeper Bruce Grobbelaar. He turned up one Christmas Eve at the midnight service. A few days later, I was to meet him at Cameron House, where he was staying with his fiancée. Later that year he invited me to a charity golf day at the Carrick Golf Course and I spent an evening with him and a host of celebrities from the world of cricket, rugby, snooker and athletics. They were having fun when I left them that night, endeavouring to drink their way through the malt whisky list of Cameron House. One for each letter of the alphabet. A for Ardbeg, B for Bunnahabhain, C for Caol Ila and so the list went on. When I left them I thought the chances of them ever reaching Tomatin or Tormore were extremely remote.

We kept in touch and he invited me out to South Africa to conduct his marriage ceremony at Stellenbosch, but it was going to be very near to Christmas. Although I would have loved to have been there, I felt it was not quite right to leave the congregation at a time so special in the church calendar.

Whenever I cease to enjoy conducting weddings, I will stop doing it. I hope and pray that that day is still far off. I have often been asked *why* I do it. There are many answers, but I have always figured that if Jesus felt it important to turn up at that wee celebration in Cana then that is a good enough reason for me to turn up when asked to officiate.

There is a serious element to a wedding: couples are taking life-changing vows. But sometimes the ceremony can be *too* serious. Even the words, 'Dearly beloved we are gathered here...' have a sombreness to them. You do not go to a wedding unless you are prepared to enjoy yourself. When Jesus was there in Cana, I have no doubt that he added to the event. Maybe his very presence made the water seem like wine.

I have had my share of comic happenings at weddings. I have had two fainters: one went down like a sack of coal, the other tumbled like a leaf falling off a tree. I have had trousers ripping - mine as I bent to retrieve the bride's ring, which the best man had dropped. I have seen a ring drop through the slats of the pier at Balmaha to be swallowed up by the waters of Loch Lomond.

My advice to anyone getting married would be to keep it simple. The more complicated it becomes, the more that can go wrong.

Two lads decided they were going to make an impressive entry on the back of a Clydesdale stallion. Either *Braveheart* or *Young Lochinvar* undoubtedly influenced them. They mounted the huge animal a mile or so from the wedding venue. Their intention was to make their stately way down from New Bonhill, across the River Leven at the Bonhill Bridge, up Bank Street into Gilmour Street and so into the Masonic Hall. I was not there to witness how they got on the horse but the saddle was at least six feet above the ground. However, I *was* there to witness the dismounting. They were a bit surprised that there was a crowd awaiting their arrival. How would they dismount while preserving their dignity? It was eventually solved by the provision of a stepladder. Hardly the image they'd had in mind.

Children never disturb me during a wedding. Left alone, they are usually fine. I have even had them creeping into the pulpit, but as long as they are safe then it's fine by me. Children cry, wail and sometimes the vows of the young couple can be completely drowned out. At such times, it has always seemed to me, the wise action would be for a parent simply to take the distressed child outside - but never, absolutely never, would I ask for a child to be removed. On one occasion, however, a mother did begin to remove her child, who was making a very modest amount of noise. I said, 'The child is not disturbing me.' At which point the retreating mother looked back at me and said quite simply, 'I think your voice is disturbing her.' And out she went.

Over the years, weddings have become more elaborate. Some have had flowers that would rival the Chelsea Flower Show. One had ten groomsmen, ten bridesmaids, four pageboys and four flower girls. Thirty-two in the wedding party once the bride, groom, best man and matron of honour were also included. The train of the bride's dress ran the whole length of the aisle. This was indeed just like the program - 'The Big Fat Gypsy Wedding'. It ticked all of the boxes except one. The bride was not exactly one of the 'travelling people'. She was over an hour late – and little wonder!

Late brides have become an epidemic. They tell me it is traditional for the bride to be late. In my book, five or ten minutes or even quarter of an hour late is fine but beyond that, unless there is some real good reason, then it's disrespectful to the guests. Of late, 20 to 30 minutes seems to be the norm. Rather than asking the usual 'Who gives this woman's hand in marriage?' at the start of the wedding, sometimes I've felt like asking, 'What kept you?'

I have had grooms faint, brides faint and wardrobe malfunctions, but I have never, in almost 4000 weddings, had either the bride or groom fail to turn up. On one occasion, it must have come close. The bride in question did not look happy. She never smiled at any point during the ceremony nor at the reception. The marriage did not last a week. Later she said, 'I knew as I walked down the aisle he was not for me.' How very, very sad.

There was one wedding that nearly did not happen because the groom was about to be arrested. His crime was that he had gone AWOL from the American naval presence at the Holy Loch. It was later revealed that he had asked permission to have time off for his wedding, but that it had been refused. So, what were his options? Risk the ire of his bride-to-be by not turning up or feel the heavy hand of the United States Navy? Personally, I think he made the safest choice. Our church officer at the time worked at the Police L division headquarters in Dumbarton. He became aware that Strathclyde's finest were being asked to support the actions of the US military police in the event of trouble at Bonhill Church. I was therefore alert and ready. I suggested to the Navy officials that if they attempted to arrest the sailor before I tied the knot then I would ensure they had front-page coverage in our national newspapers.

They relented and indicated they would wait until I had married the couple and then arrest the groom. I promised them that such a compromise might ensure the story would move from the front page to page three. I suggested that they think again and speak to their superiors in order to reach a more humane solution, which, in fairness, they did. I had the unenviable task of sharing the news with the groom that they would pick him up the following morning from the hotel where he and his new bride would be staying. He looked shell-shocked. Mind you, it was nothing to how his bride looked when two big US polis 'gate-crashed' her wedding after the legalities were completed to advise her that her honeymoon would be brief.

One groom had bought his bride to be a Ferrari as a wedding present. He and his friends were partying the night before the wedding and he had taken the car out for a spin. It careered off the road, the police were called, and he was arrested for being over the limit. He spent the night in a police cell. He kept us all waiting at the 5-star Cameron House

Hotel. His excuse was that he was hungry and 'was finishing a pie'. He was disinterested during the ceremony, but I presumed he had a lot on his mind. The hotel staff later told me that there had been a number of incidents at the reception and that the bride left for the exotic honeymoon on her own.

Before any wedding can take place, the couple MUST apply for what is called the marriage schedule. Without that piece of paper, the wedding cannot take place. I tell couples this verbally and in the detailed notes we send them, and even in a DVD that I give out for this express purpose. Yet, it is remarkable how some couples still seem to miss this important detail. Everything may be ready - photographers, videographers, the church or hotel all booked - and it can be only days or, at worst, even hours before the scheduled time that the omission is discovered.

My dilemma is that there is virtually nothing I can do. It is illegal to perform a wedding without a marriage schedule and Barlinnie Prison has never seemed appealing to me. In this situation, where I feel the omission has been a genuine (if incomprehensible) mistake, I perform a ceremony where I get them to make a promise to each another. Never at any time do I pronounce them 'husband and wife'. In those situations, most of the guests are unaware that what they are witnessing is not a wedding. They are also unaware that the couple have made a solemn promise to *me* - that they will quickly get the legal documents prepared and return a fortnight or so later so that I can marry them officially. Those poor guys now have two wedding anniversaries to remember!

There was one time, however, when I was conned. It was a big affair with some impressive guests invited. A fortnight before the wedding I checked with the groom that all was in order, including the paperwork. He feigned surprise. He claimed he knew nothing about this aspect of the arrangements. I asked him to re-read the notes we had sent him and to recall our previous conversations. I urged him to contact the Registration Office immediately and advised him that they might be able to arrange a special licence. I also contacted the registrar, who indicated that she would do all she could to help. He did not take my advice and days passed while he ignored my phone calls. He eventually indicated that he had a business to run and could not take the time off to attend to such things. The wedding seemed low in his priorities. I was faced with a dilemma: should I walk away? Probably I should have, but the human side of me wanted to save the couple from the terrible embarrassment of saying to guests, many of whom had travelled from other parts of the world, 'Sorry, no wedding, but let's party in any case.'

I held discussions with the couple and the groom promised that his priority would be to obtain the marriage schedule before going on honeymoon so that they would be officially married. He did not keep that promise. I phoned. I even drove to his house in Ayrshire in an effort to engage with him. He was always out or unavailable. A few months later I got a phone call from the police. They wanted to talk to me about a wedding. I knew immediately what was coming and was able to say, 'I did not marry them.' I could not have married them. In fact, the groom was still married.

It was a great privilege to conduct the marriages of both my sons. Derek married Natalie Campbell, a lass from Kirkintilloch. Natalie had decided she would come down the aisle to Jeremiah Clarke's trumpet voluntary but with an actual trumpet playing along with the organ. Following the American tradition, she had the bridesmaids come in first. One by one, they entered sedately, well-choreographed. Then came Natalie, looking a picture on the arm of her proud father, Douglas. As the music stopped, I could not refrain from saying, 'That was some entrance, hen.' The congregation laughed and any tensions there were just disappeared. Later they held their reception at our most favourite family lochside retreat - Ross Priory.

Andrew and Andrea were also married at the church, and what a day that was. Again, the church was packed and I doubt if there was a prouder man on the planet when Stewart escorted his beautiful daughter - looking everything a bride should look - down the aisle and handed her over to Andrew. Both weddings had the ingredients that make weddings special: laughter and tears. I provided some of the laughter and the mothers - Joan, Gill and Jacqui - the tears. Andrew acted as Derek's best man and vice versa and both showed in their respective roles that they could also be emotional. Not a bad thing. If you do not feel emotional on a day as important as your wedding, you are soul-dead. Andy and Andrea's reception took place at Kirkton House, home of the McDonalds, a marquee in the garden. Stewart and Gill were hosts par excellence. On both occasions, Natalie and Andrea decided that one day wearing the white dress was not enough, and they hosted a second reception for the members of the congregation. How they liked to party - and still do!

It is interesting that one of our sons married a Campbell and the other a McDonald. You will know that, since 1692, the two clans have not exactly got on great guns. But in this case at least, all thoughts of Glencoe have been forgotten.

On the subject of weddings, one story simply must be told. Drew Lawrie was one of the young group who came about the manse regularly. It was a real joy to be able to marry him and his lovely fiancée, Aileen Gallacher. Just before the wedding, Aileen asked if I would make sure the church bell was rung at the end of the service. I agreed; but, on the great day, I forgot to tell the church officer. It was only as bride and groom left the vestry to the tune of Mendelssohn's wedding march that I realised my omission. The bell room was at the front of the church. Sprinting up the aisle and squeezing past bride and groom was not an option. I forced open the vestry door and dashed round the side of the church, fully robed, in order to get to the front door before the bride. This being the wedding of a well-known and popular couple, I should have realised that many members of the community would be waiting outside to see the bride in all her glory. They did not expect to see Batman (robe flowing behind him) flying around the corner, so there was much laughter. I dashed into the front porch and flew upstairs before Drew and Aileen could emerge.

Reaching the bell room, I began to toll the bell. It is a big heavy bell but I soon got it going. As I did, I began to take an interest in a huge oil painting that hung in the bell-room. It showed a predecessor of mine, the Rev William Gregor. He was the minister of the parish from 1809-1840 and quite a character. Like me, William stayed around for quite some time - 31 years in fact. I got the feeling he might not have completely approved of me. I imagined he would be much more organised. He was a man of status. Anyway, I imagined the conversation that might have taken place between him and me:

HIM: 'Look at you. Call yourself a minister? I would never have been reduced to this.'

ME: 'And look at you, ye have a face there that would turn milk soor.'

In the midst of this imaginary conversation, I suddenly held onto the bell rope for too long and soared heavenwards. I then kicked on to a tall filing cabinet and stretched further up the bell rope. By this time, I was ten feet off the ground and looking down at the good cleric. I found myself saying to him, 'Bet you never did this. One up to me!'

At this point, my reverie was disturbed and the door opened. There, ten feet below me, was a 'wee wummin'. She looked at me and I looked at her. I am not often stuck for words, but I was then. I feverishly struggled to find the right way to explain my bizarre behaviour. See looked at me - fully robed on top of the filing cabinet - and solved the problem for me. She said, as if there was nothing strange in the fact that I was ten feet off the ground and hanging onto a bell rope, 'Is there a toilet in this place?' I directed her to the loo and collapsed over a table, wondering just what she might tell the other wedding guests over their steak pie.

On 1st August 2009, Joan and I celebrated our Ruby wedding. It was an interesting day. Indeed, a record for me. Through my complete inability to say no, I was landed with 5 weddings. They were all on or at Loch Lomond. Our Andy prevailed upon a friend to ferry me by fast speedboat from the Maid of the Loch to the Lodge on the Loch, then to Inchmurrin, the Cruin and eventually back to Balloch Pier. We made it

- just. Although when the engine spluttered out of fuel about 50 yards from the Balloch shoreline, I thought I might have to get out and push – or swim.

CHAPTER EIGHT

FUNERALS

TO be invited into a family home at a time of grief is a privilege I have never taken lightly. At times, I have marvelled at the ability of families to cope with the most crushing of circumstances. Their world has been torn apart, yet there can be smiles when they recount tales of laughter and fun.

In my opinion, a funeral must involve a sadness that someone so much part of a family's life is no longer with them. Yet it is also an opportunity to celebrate those memories that have been left. I suppose the saddest situation of all is when there seem to be no happy memories left behind. Thankfully, those scenarios are rare.

One incident in particular stands out in my memory. I was having great difficulty in getting the family (whom I did not know) to speak about their departed father. I probed and questioned and the answers were usually monosyllabic. Eventually, in exasperation, the son said aggressively, 'Why are you asking these questions?'

Before I could answer, the daughters, almost in unison, said, 'He wants to find something to say about our father.'

'Is that it?' he said.

I had to confess that indeed that was it.

'In which case,' he said, 'just say that he was a b******.'

The girls immediately protested that I could not say that and they began to give me something that could be fashioned into an appropriate eulogy. As I prepared to leave, the oldest daughter followed me to the door, came outside and, standing on the steps, apologised for her brother's outburst. She said, 'My father abused every single one of us, so you can imagine why we struggle to say anything positive.' She then turned, quickly re-entered the house and closed the door. No wonder it was difficult for them to talk.

Most of the time, however, I have been humbled by the stories that have poured out. Ordinary stories of happy childhoods, of simple things, of daft things but usually of parents doing the very best for their offspring. The saddest situation of all is parents talking of children who have left this world too soon.

I have always made it a rule, whenever I am given notice of a funeral, that I should make contact with the family as quickly as possible. Only once did I break that rule and thereby I learned a lesson.

The local undertaker contacted me about the death of man in New Bonhill. I made almost immediate contact with the widow and attempted to arrange a date and time to visit her. She seemed to think such a visit would be a waste of time. In any case, she was going out shopping. I indicated that the visit did not need to take place immediately, but she was strongly of the opinion that it did not need to take place at all.

There was a recurring mantra to her explanation: 'There is nothing to say about him.'

'Surely not,' I reassured her. I indicated that, as we talked, she would recall stories and incidents; tell me where he worked, what his interests were and so on. All the time she kept putting me off with the statement that it would all be a waste of time, and she could not say when she would be in - she had a lot to do.

I gave up. Probably the fact that Joan and I were about to go on holiday almost immediately after the funeral did not help. Therefore, with minimal information gleaned from three hasty phone calls, I began to take the service. During a prayer of thanksgiving, I found myself saying, 'We thank you God for the love he gave and the love he received.' The widow, sitting just three feet from the lectern, then said quite audibly, 'No' ma man.' Lesson learned.

I would seldom call without first trying to arrange a date and time that was suitable. Being unable to get a telephone response from a particular family, and realising the funeral was drawing nearer, I decided to make a visit unannounced. I climbed a few flights of stairs in a block of flats and knocked at the appropriate door, but there was no answer. I went back down the stairs and, as I was making my way to the car, there was a woman coming in my direction. She had obviously been shopping. I decided to ask her if she knew of the whereabouts of Mrs 'so and so', who lived in the block.

'That's me,' she said.

I explained who I was. Content that I now had contact, I helped her with her messages and we walked back towards her house. I was concerned that, having lost her husband, she seemed quite blasé about it all. Indeed, she warned me that her house was 'a tip'. As we entered the flat, she pointed out that it was in process of being redecorated. She need not have bothered because that was obvious – there was half-stripped wallpaper, and rolls of new wallpaper lying on a trestle table with the adhesive paste and buckets close by.

Then she said, 'He has done this to me all his life. He is always leaving jobs half finished.'

Poor soul, I thought. I am sure he would have preferred to finish the job. It was not his intention to have the heart attack that took him from us.

Ever hospitable though, the wife ushered me down the hall and then warned me there was a dog in the living room. I did not need to be warned, I could hear it and probably so could half the neighbourhood. It was desperate to get out, barking furiously and pawing at the door. Why is it that people always say, 'It will not bite you'?

When the door was eventually opened, a creature the size of a small horse came galloping towards me and the woman's declaration of its peaceful intent was of small reassurance. 'It's hungry,' the woman explained. That information did not lessen my apprehension.

'Would you feed it?' she asked.

Trying to establish a bond with this recently bereaved woman, I could hardly refuse. I did enquire where I should feed it and with what?

'In the kitchen,' she replied. Glancing around the kitchen, I could see neither a doggie bowl nor Kennomeat or whatever brand of dog food was this mutt's choice. I re-engaged with the woman who, by this time, was sitting in the living room and watching her programme of choice on television, leaving me to deal with the dancing, prancing and very hungry dog. 'I can't see anything,' I said.

'Give it cornflakes. It likes cornflakes,' she said.

'And the bowl?' I asked

'Just use your hand, it will eat out of your hand.'

I did as I was told and was glad that at the end of the exercise I still had five fingers on my right hand.

Getting down to pastoral business, I remember asking her if she was local and the answer was negative. She was more interested in the TV programme. Struggling to get her to talk, I asked her if she liked it here. Her answer was again in the negative. In a further effort to stimulate dialogue, I asked whether she might at a later stage go back to her roots. This time the response was affirmative. Thinking I had struck gold, I asked her where she was from and she answered, 'Bellsmyre'.

Bellsmyre is a housing scheme in Dumbarton. This conversation took place in a high rise flat in Braehead, Bonhill. The two communities are separated by just two large fields and the place of her birth could be seen from her living room window. At times, we can be very parochial.

One of the more intriguing incidents occurred while conducting a funeral in the Co-operative funeral parlour. During the service, I was aware there was a muttered conversation taking place in the room. I ploughed on but was becoming increasingly angry at the background of muted comments that seemed to follow my every word.

I was fuming by the end of the service and decided to watch as the mourners made their way to the cars. Last to come out were two rather unsteady individuals, still talking. Verbally, I laid into them and accused them of being disrespectful to the deceased. Suddenly one of them moved towards me, threw his arms around me and proclaimed that I was 'just magic'. The wind was taken from my sails. How could I berate someone who had given me such acclaim? I toned down my admonition but did indicate they should not talk to one another while a service was taking place.

They were suitably chastened and, by way of apology, invited me back to enjoy hospitality at a local hostelry. Having no intention of taking up this offer, I told them I still had to conduct the second part of the service at Alexandria Cemetery. At this point, they indicated they would just join me and made themselves comfortable in the back of my car. En-route, they then began to tell me just how wonderful I was - all very nice, but embarrassing and frankly untrue. To change the subject, I said, 'She was a good woman Madge.' (The name of the deceased).

From the back of the car came the question, 'Who is Madge?'

'Madge,' I said 'is the name of the woman whose funeral you have just attended.'

'Wis that who it wis?' they replied. 'That is what we were talking about. We were listening to what you were saying and trying to see if we knew her.'

'But why did you go to the funeral in the first place if you did not know who she was?' I asked. Their answer was that they had noticed some pals going in and figured that if it was someone their pals knew then they must know them as well, and of course, there was the chance that there might be a wee feed afterwards. Nothing surprises me now.

The saddest of all funerals for me have always been those for children. I still struggle. It was a happy day some years ago when I married Mark and Ann Hollern. I had known big Mark for years. It was an equally happy day when I baptised their young son, Robbie. But there were tears in my heart when I learned that Robbie had a degenerative illness. Then when his sister, Rosie, came on the scene, I was delighted again, but joy turned to sadness when I learned that she too was suffering from the same illness that had claimed Robbie a few years earlier. Mark and Ann are, however, a testimony to the triumph of the human spirit. After the loss of two children, if I had a magic wand

I would use it to wish them and their two daughters, Ruth and Roxanne, the happiest of all lives.

They appeared on the television programme *Children in Need*, appealing for funding for Robin House. It was so poignant. And, as they talked, Ruthie and Roxie played in the background. With a huge lump in my throat, I watched and listened, my heart simultaneously full of sadness, happiness and admiration.

I also find it sad when there is no one there to bid farewell. I have stood alone with perhaps only the undertaker and no other living soul. It is unbelievable that there is sometimes no one to mourn the passing of a life.

*

Funerals have become more personal in the 21st century. Music chosen often says something about the deceased. It can be tender but sometimes humorous and often expresses something of the loved one's character. We can avail ourselves of anything - *Somewhere Over the Rainbow*, *My Way*, *I'm the King of the Swingers*, *Caledonia*, *Scotland the Brave* or *Always Look on the Bright Side of Life*. Of course, for Rangers supporters, *Simply the Best*; and for the Celtic side, *The Fields of Athenry* or *You'll Never Walk Alone*. The most surprising choice, however, came in a personal request from the deceased who indicated that when the curtains closed it would be party time at a local hostelry. He also encouraged a friend, if he felt like it, to get up and dance. The piece of music was *Human* by The Killers, with its enigmatic lyrics, including *Are we human Or are we dancer?* Sure enough, as I made my exit from the crematorium there was Spit (the friend) cavorting about in front of the closing curtains.

I am often called to the bedside of those who are slipping away. Most times the patients themselves are no longer conscious and so a little prayer with the family is appropriate. Sometimes, however, the patient is very much with it. Bobby Cawley was a legend in the Vale. He was, for many years, a great friend of the late Sir Hugh Fraser, who had business interests in the Vale and was, as mentioned before, chairman of Dumbarton Football Club.

Later Bobby branched out on his own and he was a most able businessman, originally setting up a fashion shop in Alexandria. He was an ebullient personality and I reckon he would have been a success at anything he turned his hand to. He was a showman. Indeed, he was a bit of a thespian. His party song was 'Hello Dolly – it's Bobby Cawley!'

He was to buy the Duck Bay Marina and turn it into one of *the* eating-places on Loch Lomondside. That was followed by the purchase of the Gartocharn Hotel, which was renamed the Hungry Monk and subsequently became The House of Darroch. The Kirkhouse Inn, Blanefield, plus hotels in Langbank and Lochwinnoch were also part of his business portfolio. Sadly, Bobby took ill and the prognosis was not good. He called me up. As I entered the house, he said, 'Have you got a pencil?'

My reply was, 'Why?'

His answer was, 'We had better choose the hymns - for the funeral.'

He went on to give me his wish list. With a smile on his face, Bobby said, 'What I would like would be the Bonhill Pipe Band to play the cortege through the Vale. I want the crematorium to be packed to overflowing and maybe even a service in Bonhill Church.' Then he looked at me and said, 'But that is not going to happen. For the sake of my family, the funeral will be private, just the family.'

That was the way it was. Perhaps there was a notion locally that, without Bobby's charisma, his enterprises might stall. The businesses he founded, however, have gone on from strength to strength. He would be proud of his family today.

Another visit sticks out. I was asked to visit Duncan in the Western Infirmary in Glasgow. He was not a well man but his request was that I should baptise his daughters. I asked if it should it be done in the hospital but he immediately dismissed that, indicating he would be going home soon. Sadly, this was not to happen and he passed away in hospital. Funeral arrangements were made, but the night before the funeral I was summoned to the family home in New Bonhill. Finding the home was not easy. Numbers in the housing scheme are not sequential. You can spend a lifetime wondering why house number 105 does not follow 104. That night I was having trouble. Interestingly, in one of the houses there was a party going on, with the 'overflow' standing outside on the steps and in the garden. I dismissed that particular residence until one man, lager can in hand, shouted, 'There's the minister.'

Could this be the house? Indeed it was, and the 'wake' was in full swing. Unsure of what I had been called to do, I switched to ministerial mode, said a few words, concluded with a prayer and made to make my exit. In a sense, I was happy that in the oddest of circumstances I had said something, which hopefully made sense and brought comfort. I was stopped, however, by the widow, who said, 'You made a promise to Dunky. You promised to baptise the weans.'

I indicated I would be happy to fulfil that promise, but she continued: 'You said you would do it while he was here... Well he is here noo.'

And indeed he was, right there in the corner.

I often wonder how some of my colleagues might have coped with this request. But me? I baptised the weans. They were hardly weans. They were lassies ranging from 17 to 24. Lovely girls, every single one of them. The drama, however, was not quite over. Before the service started the following day, I was summoned to have a word with the widow. She told me one of her friends would sing a solo. Earlier she had indicated that there would be no hymns sung at the church, so I had not engaged an organist. Mary had the answer: 'My pal does not need an organist, she just sings from the heart.'

I did ask what her friend might sing and was assured that it would be a hymn. During the service, I cued her in. As she passed the coffin, with a nod in its direction, she said 'This is for you big man,' and launched into *One Day at a Time*, with periodic calls to the congregation to join in.

There have been funerals too of travelling people. Those funerals are often huge, with the families coming from all over Scotland to pay their respects. Some of them have been riotous, with warring factions exchanging blows. There have been times I have started only to be stopped with the information that, 'Aunty Mary is no' here yet.' There have also been times when the event has been powerful and compelling, with members of the deceased's family testifying to the power of their faith. Something akin to a religious revival seemed to be sweeping through elements of their community. Over the years, I developed a great respect for them.

In the early days, however, they were often at my door looking for money. Once they came looking for clothes, which I provided. However, on leaving they heaved the bundle back over the manse wall, leading my boys to say, 'Even the tinkers won't wear dad's cast-offs.'

There have been the tragedies. People killed by the violence of others. Anglers lost in the Loch. Children drowned in the Leven. Fathers killed in motor car accidents. A wee lad from our Sunday School sledging down a hill straight onto a road and underneath an oncoming car. The deaths of young people whom I had watched growing up through school. I have been broken as I have watched their classmates distraught and weeping uncontrollably. What do you say in the face of such grievous pain? For what it's worth, I never felt I got it right, but maybe no one could. I have also conducted far too many funerals where drug abuse has been the cause of death.

During those sad events, however, sometimes something can happen that makes it very difficult for those involved to retain their equanimity and sober countenance.

The crematorium at Cardross has a covered entrance, which has been used for years by the swallows visiting from Africa. Just as the undertakers began to wheel out the coffin, one of the swallows, perhaps in fright, deposited a little message on the undertaker's formal funeral wear.

Happy times on Loch Lomond, even in the rain.

It's Red Nose Day and we pray for a good response.

After the wedding, it's time to relax.

The annual Christmas card from the family to the congregation and friends.

All I could see was this splurge of white. I lost it. I desperately tried to regain my composure as the undertaker tried and failed to remove the evidence. It was with difficulty that I retained an air of solemnity as the cortege moved down the aisle with a rather obvious pale discolouration on the undertaker's lapel.

In the Vale of Leven cemetery there is a very quiet section, provided by the local authority, with a beautiful little memorial indicating that the garden of tranquillity was dedicated by me and my friend, Father Brendan Murtagh, late of Our Lady and St Mark's, Alexandria. SANDS - who provide emotional support to families who have endured the heartbreak of a stillbirth - provided the funding for this. It is the saddest of all things to stand with young parents whose dreams have been shattered. What should be a time of joy has turned to one of sadness. For months they will have been filled with excitement - will have talked about the changes the birth of a might bring about and probably argued over names. For them the sun has been shining. And then, suddenly, there is overwhelming darkness. Undertakers, gravediggers, crematorium attendants... I hope that clergy are ultra-sensitive in such situations.

I have so many of those little moments fixed poignantly in my mind. I often pause a while when passing through a cemetery - I read the names and remember the losses of those families. They may have moved on, but never completely. Their pain remains.

I remember one such event for all the wrong reasons. There is always a great willingness among all parties to be especially respectful. I am sure that it was with this in mind that one of our young undertakers stepped back with great decorum to allow me to continue with the service. There had been a lot of rain and there was a steep slope behind the little grave. Suddenly I saw Alasdair slipping down the slope with increasing rapidity. He looked for all the world like someone on a fast treadmill trying to keep up but failing. Arms flailing, desperation on his face, and almost bent double, he was scrambling. His desperation was soon replaced by terror - it would hardly be the thing for the mourning family to see the undertaker carried away in an avalanche of mud. They were looking towards me, unaware of the drama, but I could see it all. How I managed to get through that service without exploding is one of life's wonders.

For the mourners the only event in the world that matters at that moment is their saying farewell to their loved one. Understandably, nothing else features in their universe. However, the world continues to spin. The crematorium staff, the undertakers and sometimes even the minister have their schedules.

It has become the practice that at the end of the service, especially at the crematorium, people shake hands with all who have attended. This can take anything from 10 to 30 minutes. Now and again this creates a problem - for example, if another bereaved family is waiting to gain access to the service room. Usually all that is required is a very gentle reminder from the staff, coupled with the suggestion that any conversations could perhaps continue at the reception venue. The crowd generally disperses within a few minutes. But not always.

One memorable moment in this regard will remain with me. The family showed no sign of moving on even though the cortege for the next family was waiting. I tried to very gently engage with the hand shakers but they looked through me without a word. Five minutes later, I tried again. Again, no more than a disdainful look. The crematorium staff received the same non-compliance. Eventually, anger took control and I just said, 'Sorry I am not asking you, I am telling you to MOVE - the next funeral should have started 10 minutes ago.' They slowly moved away while giving me the sort of look normally reserved for something crawling out of a swamp.

Outside, the conversations continued, thereby preventing the arrival of the next cortege. It's the only time I have ever been angry at the flagrant lack of respect shown for another distressed family. I strode in again. I should not have, but I did. Very pointedly I explained that, in the black cars, which were clearly visible, was a grieving family facing an ordeal and being delayed by the contemptuous disregard being shown to them. In a very plummy, public school voice, a young man turned to me and said, 'But she was an opera singer.' Obviously, in the mind of the speaker, that excused ignorance. I decided any response that I felt like making would be singularly inappropriate.

Fellow clergy and other celebrants are not entirely without blame. At Cardross, there was an hour gap between services. More than enough time for the service, 15 minutes to allow the mourners to disperse and fifteen minutes for the next family to arrive. As always, the most important people are the bereaved, but they are usually open to advice. If someone – be they a member of the family or a friend - is going to deliver a eulogy, then any minister, priest or celebrant should be able to tailor what he says accordingly. Sadly, not all do. Not to do so causes pressure on the undertakers, crematorium staff and often on other families.

I always counsel that those tasked with delivering the eulogy should have it written down. That way, in the event of them finding the occasion too much, I am able to step in. Not everyone follows that advice.

People fall into three categories. There are those who are aware of what they are going to do and who do it well but not without emotional difficulty. Then there are those who just find the occasion too much. They see the crowd and freeze or they stumble through it with tears and apologies, but in the main that also works, especially when sincerity shines through. The final category is those who 'speak from the heart'. Sometimes the fact that they become the centre of attention appeals. The fact that they have written nothing down makes them akin to an unexploded bomb.

One young man got up to speak. He had obviously taken something to give him courage. He started with much bending of his knees and some 'interesting' facial expressions. His opening line was, 'Well what can I say?' If he did not know the answer to that question then we were in trouble. Eventually he told a few inappropriate stories, mostly involving drink, before saying, 'Remember what he always said when you came into the house - shut the door - pit oot the light.' Strolling over to the coffin, he struck the lid and said, 'Well your light is oot noo.'

He was not finished. Addressing the congregation, he said, 'Thanks for coming, but I just want to ask where you were when he was ill?' Actually, the whole thing was sprinkled with expletives that I have omitted. At the end of it all, I found myself saying to the assembled company, most of whom were gazing at the floor, 'Well, that was, eh...different.'

On the other hand, I have listened to so many wonderful, sensitive, poignant and beautiful eulogies. Often I have found myself saying, 'No-one could have done it better.'

For me, it has been a very humbling privilege to be part of their family, often expressing the thoughts they feel unable to share. Many of their memories are too touching to recall. Then there is the laughter, and sometimes the daft stories that even they were not sure should be told. In 40 years of ministry, I have now conducted over 5,000 funerals. For some that might seem to be a burden. For others maybe it seems like a commitment that has meant other plans must have had to be shelved. For me, it has been a privilege I would not have missed for all the world.

CHAPTER NINE

FINAL YEARS AND RETIREMENT

WHEN do you retire? The best advice I ever got was from the Presbytery Clerk, my friend the Rev David Clark: 'Go when they are asking, WHY? Not when they are asking, WHEN?' I hope I got it right.

None of us can claim immortality, though at times I had the tendency to think I could. In my mid-sixties rationality began to kick in. My worst fear was that my exit from this world would leave Joan having, in due course, to vacate the manse. It seemed wiser that the decision to move should be taken when we were both reasonably fit. A decision taken by choice rather than necessity.

Andrew and Andrea were moving to Cardross. The project was to convert the large former farmhouse - the residence of Andrea's parents - into two separate dwellings. This has been done so tastefully. It suited Stewart and Gill not to move from a house they love and allowed Andy and Andrea to live in a superb house with fabulous views of the Clyde and the mountains of Argyll. I decided to buy back 'Derand' when Andy and Andrea moved on, so that in the future we would have a roof over our heads.

I retained great enthusiasm for the church and parish but David's wise words about *Why?* and *When?* struck a chord. At the same time, the Planning Committee of the Presbytery had been instructed to reduce the number of ministers in our area and to link Bonhill with Renton Church. I felt my departure would help to expedite such a plan.

In the spring of 2012, I made the decision and announced that on the 30th of June of that year I would cease to be the minister at Bonhill Church. This decision was not taken lightly and only after much heart-searching and regret, but after 37 wonderful years I felt it was right for Bonhill, for Joan and for myself.

During those 37 years, I enjoyed the wholehearted support of a wonderful congregation. I had the loyalty of a great bunch of office-bearers. We may not always have agreed, but I like to think the words I spoke at the beginning of my ministry - 'We will do this together or we won't do it at all' - were as valid at the end of my ministry as they were at its beginning in 1975.

As I look back, I consider myself incredibly fortunate. I had very few major disagreements with members of the congregation and those minor fallouts were soon attended to, with friendships restored almost without exception. Almost, but sadly not quite.

The last year of my ministry was clouded. It involved the parting of the ways between the church, Andrew our treasured organist and my friend, and myself.

Andrew was one of the mainstays of the congregation, serving over the years as Session Clerk, being part of the rebuild project team and certainly someone who could be relied upon to come up with innovative ideas and plans and see them through. He was also our very accomplished organist. He was an integral part of all that happened at Bonhill Church.

Andrew began to feel unhappy about certain changes that had happened involving music. Attempts were made to seek a compromise. I had many meetings in an attempt to keep him on board. He was my friend. Indeed, I had been his best man. His parents and sister were the very best of folk. Eventually, I had to accept that finding a resolution - a compromise - appeared to be beyond my ability, and that the matter should be taken out of my hands and handed over to the Kirk Session to resolve. The eventual outcome was that Andrew resigned. It was one of the saddest moments of my time at Bonhill. He was a friend - a colleague with whom I had shared so many happy times. I can only conclude that it was one of those situations in which both sides could see the issue in clear terms. Thus they thought that the solution was simple. The problem was that their solutions were diametrically opposed. Sometimes there are just no answers as to why such things happen, and perhaps what some see as a matter of principle others would see as something not worth fighting over. I can only conclude that this was just such a situation.

Carol McLean was persuaded to take on the job of organist, although she needed some persuading. However, she has also become a very loyal and faithful servant to the church. Her ability to inspire folk to sing is remarkable. Carol was a member of the famous Dalvait Singers, whose conductor was the charismatic Jean Graham. Jean would be very proud of her 'pupil'.

There was also fun in the run-up to my departure. The church was used now and again to film funerals for the BBC television soap *River City*. Actors, extras, equipment and even buses kitted out as cafeterias would surround the church. On one occasion, I stopped while they were setting up, parked the car at the top of the driveway, jumped out and ran down towards the church. I grabbed something from the church office and ran back out again towards the car. An official stopped me and asked where I was going, sayingsaid that I would soon be called onto the set. I had been mistaken for the actor who was about to conduct the *River City* funeral. I had to say to him, 'No, I am the real thing.'

It was obvious the congregation wanted to do something to celebrate the fact that, at last, I was going. In an incredible act of kindness and generosity, they bought Joan and me two tickets for the Orient Express to Venice and three nights at the Hotel Cipriani, where George Clooney had his honeymoon. It is very posh indeed. Joan and I flew from Edinburgh to Venice and then we got the water-taxi into St Mark's Square, where we were picked up by the very plush launch sent especially from the hotel. The Cipriani was quiet and tasteful. Staying there was a once-in-a-lifetime experience.

Then we made our way back on the Orient Express, looking around with trepidation in case a quaint little Belgian gentleman called Poirot was on board.

The carriages were a reminder of how the rich and famous used to travel. They have been restored to their former glory but not changed to accommodate the expectations of 21st century luxury. Toilets are still at the end of the corridor. However, the attention to detail, the food and the service are simply the best. There are no 'en-suite facilities' but also no air conditioning, so it can get warm - very warm, indeed excruciatingly so.

Our personal attendant ran backwards and forwards bringing us cloths soaked in ice-cold water but the heat continued as we made our way through Northern Italy and Austria and into Switzerland. At one of the stops, right beside Lake Wallenstein, the couple in the next compartment jumped off the train and dived straight into the lake. That was one way to cool off.

As darkness fell, the heat and humidity persisted. Even the advent of an electrical storm did little to lower the temperature, but we watched an amazing display of heavenly pyrotechnics lighting up the lake, mountains and villages as we made our way through Switzerland. We wined and dined and felt like royalty, our every whim indulged.

After dinner, we returned to our compartment, which was transformed for our night's sleep. Joan chose the bottom bunk and I the top. It was still torrid. I kicked off all the coverings. I managed to get the fan going, blowing colder air into the sauna of our bedroom. It began to cool and we both fell asleep, helped, I suppose, by the rocking movement of the train.

The fan continued to blast cold air onto my head. I did ask my dear wife in the lower bunk if I should turn it off and her reply was in the negative. By this time, I was beginning to freeze. From the tropics to the Antarctic in a matter of moments. I covered up with the discarded blankets and began to feel like Nanook of the North. However, I slept and then through my stupor I heard a persistent knocking. I presumed something had come loose in the little cubicle that housed a wash hand basin. I ignored it and covered up in my igloo.

The knocking continued, but with long intervals of silence. Could it be Joan out in the corridor? I looked down at the lower bunk and convinced myself that my beloved was still in the land of nod. The knocking continued. I had a flashback to my school days listening to Macbeth - 'Wake Duncan with thy knocking.' It was waking me all right. Glasses on, I peered down again and - no Joan! Feverishly, I opened the compartment door and there she was in all her bath-robed glory. Having left to answer the call of nature, the door had closed behind her and she had spent over half an hour making nodding acquaintance with those on a mission similar to her own.

However, what memories of a wonderful gift and an amazing journey on one of the world's iconic trains. Our over-generous congregation also gave us matching Rotary watches.

Saturday the 30th of June 2012 was officially my last day as the minister of the parish. A farewell concert was held in a packed church of almost 400 parishioners. It was a full house, with a waiting list of those who wished to come. It was a wonderful concert. Many of my friends participated and, of course, you cannot put a good man down, so I made my own contribution. Singing a little ditty that used to be sung by Willie Barclay's choir...

> 'The minister, the session clerk, the beadle.
> Good men and true you'll agree.
> The minister, the session clerk, the beadle.
> The men that run the Kirk, we three.'

We had Malcolm McKay, looking like a more realistic minister than the one retiring; Willie Murray as a very severe Session Clerk; and me as the Beadle.

I ended the concert by giving a closing epilogue or Late Call, à la Rikki Fulton. It went down a treat with almost everyone. There was just one exception. Ben Miller, who was just five at the time, did say, 'When is he going to finish?' I wonder how often some of the long-suffering members of the congregation said that?

One contribution brought the house down. Rosie Green sang the first verse of *Me and My Teddy Bear*. Then, during the second verse, she was joined by Ben Miller, who clutched a teddy bear as he descended the pulpit stairs and joined Rosie in the song. He had been hiding. It had all been kept secret from me.

We all have our *'bucket lists'*. One of mine was to sing in a Welsh male voice choir and I was able to do that down in Chepstow when I sang with the choir there. Another was to sing with a local band, The Executives. I wanted to sing along with them in harmony in a rendition of *Hello Mary Lou*. At a wedding reception, and live on local radio, we did it. Ricky Nelson had nothing on us.

A few weeks later, I got an invite to be part of a 'Kirkin' of the Council' at Bonhill Church. I was no longer the minister and it would not normally be considered appropriate for me to return. The Rev Barbara O'Donnell was now acting as locum and she graciously allowed me to preach the sermon whilst she conducted the service. During the service, Provost Douglas McAllister announced that the council had decided to award me the honour of becoming a Freeman of Dumbarton.

I was speechless and very emotional. It is an honour I share with some remarkable people. People like Sir Jackie Stewart and Robert Burns. It now means I can graze my cows on Dumbarton Common. If only I had any.

Very generously, the Council hosted a civic reception for me. They asked me to invite family and friends. They suggested I give every table a special name and I did. People who have in their own way contributed to our community and often to the wider world.

1. **Tobias Smollett** was educated at the University of Glasgow, qualifying as a surgeon. His career in medicine, however, came second to his literary ambitions, and in 1739, he went to London to seek his

fortune as a dramatist. The Adventures of Roderick Random made his name. He was recognised as a leading literary figure of his time.

2. **Robert Nairn** was a shoemaker in Bonhill and a covenanter who stood for religious freedom. His principles caused him to abstain from church attendance, which was at the time a criminal offence, so he had to leave home and hide in the Dalmonach woods. The cumulative effects of 'living rough', caught up with him, and he died on 15th April 1685. The minister of the time refused him burial. Some of his friends entered the Kirkyard and buried him under cover of darkness.

3. **Lachie Stewart** is best known for winning the gold medal for the 10,000 metres race at the 1970 Commonwealth Games in Edinburgh in a thrilling finish against Ron Clarke of Australia. Lachie was brought up in the Dalmonach Estate and as a young man his training routine was running on the hills above the golf course. In that famous race, he sped past Clarke on the back straight to finish a clear winner in front of an ecstatic Meadowbank crowd. Lachie is just one of nature's gentlemen. A humble, lovely man.

4. **Dan O'Hare** was one of the outstanding political figures of the 20th century in the Vale of Leven. He was victimised by his employers for his trade union and political activities. He served for many years as a Communist councillor. Given his contribution to the improvements in the Vale, it was appropriate that not just a street but a whole estate was named after him – the O'Hare Estate, Bonhill. Dan was a man of independent mind. In Jim Bollan today we have his successor.

5. **Peter Haining** learned to row at the Loch Lomond Rowing Club, a club that produced many Scottish Champions like Jim McNiven, Jim Paton and John McArthur. Peter Haining accumulated many medals and won the World Sculling Championship title three years in succession. He was also awarded the CBE.

6. **Charlene Spiteri** was raised in Balloch. She said her surroundings provided her with outdoor adventuring, and the fractured wrist, finger and four broken noses she suffered throughout her childhood are a testament to that. She was a member of a musical family. The Spiteri household was often filled with the sounds of rock and soul. She is the lead singer of Texas.

7. **Neil McCallum** was to score the first goal for Celtic, on 28th May 1888. He was born in Bonhill in 1869, died aged 51 in 1920, and was buried in Bonhill Churchyard. Neilly was a member of the 1888 Renton World Champions team when only 19. As well as Renton and Celtic, Neil played for Blackburn Rovers, Nottingham Forest and Notts County before going back to the Celtic fold. Appropriately, The Celtic Graves society recently marked his last resting place.

8. **Ernie Miller** was not a Vale man, unlike all the others. He was born in Kilbarchan, moving to Greenock and then returning to Kilbarchan at the time of the Greenock blitz. Yet he chose to move to the Vale in 1982 and spent almost 20 happy years there. Indeed, he would consider the times spent - especially with his grandchildren - the happiest of his life. He had strong views on many things, though as a committed Christian he was strongly against bigotry and discrimination of any kind and was a life-long pacifist. He was gifted musically and had both a wonderful sense of humour and endless patience. He was an ordinary man of extraordinary qualities.

9. **Sir John Pender** was a Bonhill lad who went on to find fame and fortune as an entrepreneur. His greatest success came in the early stages of telecommunications. The cable business he created connected all corners of the British Empire and beyond. He also had a political career as a Liberal. He is the only Vale man to appear in the National Gallery.

10. **Alexander Tait,** aka Willie Scobie, is well known as a local historian and novelist. His latest offering *Upon This Rock* (a story that centres round Dumbarton Rock) has been described as follows: 'This book has it all - romance, subterfuge, and adventure. It is set amidst an important era of Scottish history and manages to both educate and excite. It is especially relevant in an age where religious bigotry still raises its head. As befits all good books, the ending is especially worth waiting for!'

Agnes Owen is another local author. Also into the category of contemporary novelists is Sam Wilding aka **Paul Murdoch**. Paul is also a gifted musician and humanitarian. He wrote his first novel *The Magic Scales* in 2006 and many have followed since. The literary tradition started by Tobias Smollett is alive and well.

11. **Ian McColl** was born in the Vale. He played for the Vale Juniors and then, in 1943, joined Queen's Park. In 1945 he was signed by Bill Struth for Glasgow Rangers. He made 526 appearances for the Glasgow club and won 14 caps for Scotland. He then went into management. He was appointed manager of Scotland in 1960 and was in charge for 27 matches. His brother-in-law, Jim McLean, still lives locally. Ian was not the only famous footballer of recent times from the Vale. We can add the names of Bobby Kerr and John O Hare.

12. **Ben, Josh, Rowan and Jake Miller.** Many of the tables bear the names of those who have contributed to our community or history, but not Ben, Josh, Rowan or Jake. They have done nothing of note, being aged six, three, two and one at the time, but they represent the future. May our local authority continue to ensure our children have the best of educations and safest of environments in which to live. May our politicians ensure that the best of healthcare is available to all. Working together they can – and must - ensure that for future generations West Dumbarton continues to be a good place to live.

13. **Tini Black** was a Vale character, a worthy who was known for her rough voice and distinctive appearance. She was once evicted from her council house and appeared on national television. She was quick to point out that she was not evicted for non-payment of rent. The eviction was for, in her own words, 'DURT'. She was warm-hearted and was well known for speaking to every bairn as she made her way along Main Street. Long may the characters remain, bringing life and laughter to all who know them.

14. **Jimmy Kerr** was also a character. He represents the countless people who worked on the QE2 and claimed to have built it single-handed! What a pride that group of workers took in their trade. No wonder the term *Clydebuilt* stood for quality. Like his friend Tom Weir, Jimmy loved the outdoors and was committed to protecting the environment long before environmental issues were in vogue. Jimmy's opinions were often different from those of his peers but he enjoyed justifying them in debate. He left us a few years ago, just short of his 100th birthday.

The council handed me a scroll that said the bestowing of this honour was...

'In recognition of his distinguished service and commitment to the communities of Bonhill, of the Vale of Leven and of West Dunbartonshire as a whole, and in appreciation of his significant contribution to the social wellbeing of the people of this area; for his dedication to public and voluntary service through his membership of the local health trust, former health board and the West Dunbartonshire Social Work Complaints Review Subcommittee; for his participation in the education of children; and in recognition of the tremendous amount of work which he selflessly undertook as minister for the people of Bonhill Parish; for his support of local charities; and in honour of his personal qualities, his humour and the respect maintained for him.'

Like anyone who receives any kind of honour there is a feeling of unworthiness. Listening to the kind things people say is almost like hearing your own funeral eulogy and thinking *that is not really me*. Though I felt unworthy, I also felt immensely proud that the piper Colin Lawrie had recommended me for this honour and that the councillors considered me worthy.

*

Other surprises were in store. One day a phone call informed me that I was being invited by HM the Queen to spend the weekend at Balmoral and to preach at Crathie Church on the Sunday morning. I suppose I asked the question that anyone would ask, 'Why me?' One of the officials told me that Her Majesty enjoyed coming to Scotland and hearing *'ordinary ministers'*. I remember saying to the caller, 'In which case, I qualify.'

The appointed date was 12th August. As it drew near, I began to become apprehensive. I should not have worried. The Royal Family were incredibly warm and hospitable. I was left with the overwhelming feeling that they were very normal. Now I know that sounds mad, but it's true. They made me feel very much at home. I have many memories of that occasion, including that the Queen has a most dazzling smile and very quick sense of humour, and that the Duke is knowledgeable and loves conversing. I also remember when I sat in the front seat of the Range Rover as she drove me to a barbecue. It was quite surreal. Her Majesty just talked as naturally as she negotiated the rutted roads of the Balmoral estate - one eye on me and one on the road. Alex Salmond later commented that he had a similar experience during just such a journey.

What came to me very strongly was just how much the royals love Scotland and how happy they are at Balmoral, where they are away from prying eyes and can be themselves.

On the Sunday, I went with the Rev Ken MacKenzie, minister of Crathie, and took the service at Braemar. Obviously Ken felt that perhaps there was something unique in my style. Introducing me to the congregation of Crathie and the Royal Family, he just said, 'Hold onto your seats.'

My sermon centred on the need for us to take a risk now and again. There were two readings, one concerning the feeding of the 5,000 and the other the incident when Peter stepped out of the boat and walked on the water.

My starting point for the sermon was the whole issue of miracles. I suggested that many of the miracles Jesus performed would today be viewed with suspicion. Here is an abridged version of the script from which I read that day.

We live in a wonderful and incredible world. We can watch things in our living rooms that our forefathers could never have dreamed about. It is amazing, yet we are sceptical about the miraculous. You might be sceptical about the miracles we read about this morning. On the other hand, you might just simply ask what relevance they have for us.

If you feel it could not happen today you are probably right.

Turning water into wine would provoke outrage from the drinks industry.

Feeding the multitude at an outdoor event would require the approval of government health inspectors.

Walking on water should only be done if preceded by the warning that nobody should try it at home.

Healing a man born blind could lead to all sorts of problems. All disability benefits would be stopped, and the man in question probably investigated as to whether his previous claims had been genuine.

As for raising the dead... Environmental health would not be happy. There would also be major problems when the recently deceased tried to use his credit cards.

Yes, miracles would be up against it today.

However, they were also up against it in Jesus' day. I am sure the disciples thought Jesus had lost it when he asked them to feed the crowd. They were for sending folk home. They said it could not be done! Impossible! That attitude still exists when someone tries something different.

Isn't that true no matter what we try to do in life? There is always someone saying, 'You can't do that.' And so it was in Jesus' day. Jesus told the disciples to give the crowd something to eat and they said, 'We have here only five loaves and two fishes.'

Jesus took those five loaves and the two fishes and everyone was fed. How did it happen? Some believe the crowd brought food with them. They had kept it hidden until this wee laddie offered to share his picnic and thereby shamed the others into offering theirs.

But what of walking on water? I am sure that you have heard the story of the tourist who visits the Holy Land. One night, he decides to take his wife on a boat trip. He asks the man in charge how much it will cost. The man says 'Twenty-five US dollars.' The tourist walks away and says, 'Now I know why Jesus walked.' However, behind the joke again is this notion that we know what is possible and we know what is impossible. Tthat is why we have problems with miracles and why we are probably averse to taking risks.

Peter took a risk. He acted without thinking. You and I know folk like that. They think more with their heart than with their head. But Jesus loved Peter. With all his impulsiveness, all his bravado, all his enthusiasm, Jesus loved Peter. Even though he was always putting his foot in it, and even though he nearly drowned this time, Jesus loved him. He saw him as a man who was willing to take a risk for his faith.

Do you think that the Good Samaritan became good by playing it safe? He took a risk. Peter could have stayed in the boat. However, we would not be hearing about him today. Now of course there is a place for caution in life. By praising Peter, I am not suggesting that we forget common sense. There are risks we should not take. But now and again, we need to take a risk. We need to take a chance. There comes a time when you must step out of the boat.

WITHOUT RISK TAKERS, THE WORLD WOULD NEVER MOVE FORWARD. No one would ever do anything at all if we took risk-taking out of life. All of us take risks. Nothing would happen if we did not. No new relationships would be formed. No new businesses would be started. No new homes would be built. Helen Keller got it right when she said that, 'Life is either a daring adventure or nothing.'

The Duchess of Wessex had expressed the hope, at dinner the night before, that 'I was not a long-winded preacher.' I did not disappoint her. I did suggest to her that if I went beyond a certain time in the pulpit, she should cough. She did say later, 'You did not hear me coughing.' That characterized the open, easy and friendly way they made me feel at home.

After the service, I had the great pleasure of meeting John Edrich, an elder at Crathie. John was a hero of mine, an opening batsman for Surrey and England.

One of the younger royals later asked for a copy of my sermon. I wondered whether they were just being kind and, on returning home, I felt it would be a bit presumptuous of me to send up the sermon. However, later in the week, I received a phone call wondering where the missing sermon was.

My mother passed away in 1996. In some ways, the memories she left me are always there, but in my bedroom at Balmoral, I just had this overwhelming wish that she could see me. Could God just grant me five minutes so that she could see where her boy was? Perhaps she knew.

There was one more honour to come before the year was over. As a life-long Celtic supporter, the fact that Neil McCallum was buried in Bonhill was a matter of great significance to me. I got involved with the Celtic Graves Society. They invited me to speak at the 125th birthday of that great club. On the 6th November 2012, I spoke to a packed St

Mary's Church in Calton where Brother Walfrid founded the club to help the disadvantaged poor of the East End of the city.

What an honour for a Protestant clergyman to be granted the privilege of speaking on that historic occasion. The following day the the press wrote :

'St Mary's Church was at capacity for last night's anniversary celebrations and Mass, with manager Neil Lennon in attendance alongside club directors, chief executive Peter Lawwell and Celtic's majority shareholder, Dermot Desmond.

The pews were also packed with former players, with the Lisbon Lions sitting alongside Danny McGrain, Davie Hay, Tom Boyd, George McCluskey and Dutch striker, Jan Vennegoor of Hesselink - as well as some of the Barcelona directors - who will watch their side run out at Celtic Park in the Champions League tomorrow. They were welcomed as guests of honour in an opening address by club chairman, Ian Bankier, who also spoke of Celtic's heritage as 'a Glasgow club with Irish roots'.

The other speakers also highlighted this history, with Church of Scotland minister and Celtic supporter, Ian Miller stealing the show'.

In my speech, I mentioned my life-long support of the team and that I had a foot in 'the other camp'. I mentioned my connection with Walter Smith. Before the Mass, Father Thomas White also mentioned Walter and disclosed that when he was a boy living in Carmyle, Walter let him drive his Volkswagen round the Oval.

Celtic and Scotland hero Murdo Macleod was running me home and phoned Walter, who told him he had already had a text from someone at the Mass, so he said, 'There were many great luminaries of Celtic's past who did not get a mention but I got mentioned twice!' This was Scottish humour at its best. Walter Smith is a man of integrity and honesty and this has been borne out during Rangers difficulties in the past few years. In truth, he is 'Simply the Best'.

And so a very eventful year came to an end.

CHAPTER TEN

PEOPLE

THE newspaper article proclaimed, 'A Scottish village is bracing itself for a gold rush after £200 million of the precious metal was discovered in its hills. The popular tourist village of Tyndrum is believed to have more of the rare metal than previously thought'. A television programme followed with the catch phrase, 'there is gold in them thar hills'.

Well for me it was not gold in the hills but gold in the valley, and the gold was its people. It was the warmth of the people of the Valley of the Leven that brought me to Bonhill and the warmth of the people who kept me there for my entire ministry and beyond. They did not put me on a pedestal and I did not want to be on one. They accepted me and my family as one of their own. Without them, our life would have been much the poorer.

There were the odd ones who made life more difficult and challenging - those who would phone any time day or night, usually under the influence of alcohol, and those who would come to the door looking for money with the most incredible stories. If they called me Rev Miller, I used to reckon they were looking for £100; those who called me Rev Ian were much more modest in their expectations; and the ones who just called me Ian were generally looking for nothing.

One parishioner took to phoning me in the middle of the night without speaking. The police were able to trace the call but legitimately felt that it helped no one for them to tell me the name of the caller. At least it stopped the calls.

One of the most interesting situations developed when a new member came to the church and became involved, arranging trips and fundraising events. But, as always, there was a cost. She expected me to be involved in all of her plans. When I indicated that maybe I had other priorities, but was happy for her to continue, things became frosty. I would be besieged by letters accusing me of all sorts of things.

I began to get bills from local florists for flowers I had sent to her, even though. I had sent no such flowers. One Sunday morning a singing telegram appeared in church. His mission was to sing to me a song from my 'girlfriend'. Thankfully, office-bearers were able to head this off, but by this time, I was alarmed. Things came to a head when *The Sun* newspaper turned up after a service, claiming I was having an affair with the woman. Office-bearers alerted me to the presence of photographers in the churchyard, so I made a hasty exit out of a side door and headed to the manse. My two boys at this time told me that a reporter had been at the door. I am glad their response was not recorded.

I phoned the editor and asked him to tell his reporters to knock on the doors of every house on Main Street, Bonhill; if one person indicated that there might be some truth in the allegation I would then talk to them. They never returned. They did, however, manage to contact Joan. They asked her, 'Do you not think he is capable of having an affair?' Her answer, was 'Really, I do not know whether he has the inclination or not, he certainly does not have the time.' So no headlines for me in *The Sun*. There was just a brief mention under the heading *Weirdo Makes Rev's Life Hell*.

The story did not end there because eventually there was a headline in *The Sun* involving the same woman and another minister. I suppose it is the sort of thing faced by ministers, doctors and those in other professions.

Over the years, I have been indebted to many who have encouraged, supported, changed, taught and inspired me. People like Elaine McGeachie, who courageously fought leukaemia for many years and established a 'prayers for healing' group in our church with a number of friends at which many people found, and still do find, great solace.

People like the Campbell Clan who adopted me as their *'chaplain'*.

I would rarely conduct a funeral or wedding without a salmon mysteriously turning up on the doorstep or in the back seat of my car. No questions asked and no answers given.

People like Tom Glen, my first neighbour in Bonhill, who lived to be 101 and was on the ball until the end. He became a great friend and inspiration and later his son, Noel, continued that tradition.

People like Nina McGregor who produced many a hilarious play in the church hall, with some real ham actors including me.

Then there are Willie Murray, Stan Jones and Jim Mclean who introduced me to the game of golf that I still play erratically but enthusiastically.

In fact, the list is just endless and includes generous people and humorous people. I was once held in custody in a cell in the appropriately named Hill Street Police Station. I should explain that I had done nothing wrong - the organisers of the Anthony Nolan bone marrow trust were phoning local business people asking if they would contribute £50 to their fund, the idea being that I would be released if the desired amount was raised. Allan Wright, well-known entrepreneur and Rangers man, came round to the police station with £250 and said, 'I will give you this if you keep him in.'

Weddings and baptisms brought me into contact with Kelly McDonald and Robert Carlisle. Speaking engagements found me sitting beside Prince Andrew and Viv Richards.

I found myself wishing I could have met Mary Stewart instead of finding myself conducting her funeral. I read so many of Mary's books as a young man -- *The Wicked Days*, *The Crystal Cave*, *The Hollow Hills* and many more. Mary passed away in Oban at the grand old age of 97. One critic said of her, 'She arguably inspired the deluge of best-selling romantic fiction that has flooded the market in recent decades. During a writing career of more than 40 years, she produced a score of chart-topping novels that sold in excess of five million copies and made her an international household name.'

I would love to have met her but her niece was able to tell me a quite wonderful story about her Aunt Mary. They were obviously very close and often spent the evening chatting to one another. During one of those conversations Mary said, 'What day is today?'

On being told that it was Thursday she then said, 'No, I mean what date is it?'

She was told it was the 8th of May and then she said, 'On the 9th of May, Fred came calling. I think he is calling me again.' Fred was her late husband, a former Professor of Geology at Edinburgh University. She went to her bed and during the night left us to re-join the love of her life.

Fred had been knighted, and so technically Mary was a Lady, though she never used the title. Her niece told me he used to say to her, 'Well Mary, at last I have managed to make you a lady.'

I just wish I had met her in life.

*

One of the best decisions taken by the church was to have a fully functioning office and a secretary who would organize the place; and, maybe more importantly, organize me. Into the breach stepped Alice McWilliam, who became the first port of call for anyone seeking information about Bonhill Church, weddings, funerals, baptisms, my availability and so on. Alice became integral to my ministry. She had the most important quality for anyone working with me and that was a sense of humour, often an irreverent one. The church office became a place of work but also of laughter. There is a notice that Alice stuck on the wall. It remains there to this day and it simply states, 'Many people bring joy to this place, some by their arrival and some by their departure.' The truth of that statement also remains.

One day someone came to the office with a gift - a watercolour painting of the Madonna and child looking down on Bonhill Church. The benefactor had long reddish hair and I pigeonholed him as a bit of a hippy. He came, he gave and he left. He did not leave his name, but I did notice on the painting, which I put up on the church hall wall, the name Scobie. End of story I thought. Some ten years or so later I got a phone call from someone who enquired about joining the church. I met him and he introduced himself as Willie Scobie. We agreed that he should join in a simple ceremony, which I and my colleague Ken Russell attended. I was to get to know Willie over the next few months and, at one point, I referred to the painting gifted to the church, obviously painted by someone called Scobie... Maybe a relative? I enquired.

'I painted the picture,' came back the reply. He had changed just a little bit. The long hair had gone and what was left was definitely thinning. Thus started a friendship between me and this remarkable man.

I would concede that Willie is 'different'. Willie was a bachelor in his mid- to late-forties when he took the plunge into matrimony with Mary at St Mahew's Church in Cardross. Willie is now father to his three dearly loved children, probably at an age when some men are thinking 'pipe and slippers'.

Willie is unique. He has a plethora of interests. He is knowledgeable about most things, but especially Scottish History (especially Local History) and Literature. He is a painter, poet and author. He designed a new stained glass window for Bonhill Church; he composed a new hymn for Easter and, as my retirement approached, designed, without my knowledge, a tartan and registered it with the Scottish Register of Tartans as the Rev Ian Miller tartan, which I now proudly wear. Yes, I have met some amazingly talented people in my life and Willie is certainly one of them.

*

The second-best decision in my life was coming to the Vale of Leven. The best was, of course, marrying Joan. From the very outset she let it be known that she had no intention of sitting in the 'manse pew'. It was the tradition that the minister's family was given a special seat. This was not for her. Furthermore, she would state in her own quiet way that she happened to be the wife of Ian Miller and not 'the minister's wife'. She was a member of the congregation and as such took part in congregational activities but not as 'my wife'. She is simply known by all as Joan. She has never got involved in church politics, never caused any trouble or friction, but has been quick to say to me, if I've been about to embark impetuously on some course of action, 'Go and pour yourself a drink and do what you need to do tomorrow.' By that time, I've been less likely to take erratic action.

Weddings have become so much part of my life, yet when it is at your own door it is different. It was a privilege to marry both Derek and Natalie and Andy and Andrea. It was touching to hear what they had to say. Derek would have preferred to have remained silent but he acquitted himself well and with sincerity said:

'*Without Douglas and Jacqui Campbell and Ian and Joan Miller this day would not have happened. They should both know we appreciate the part that both sets of parents have played. Much more importantly, we know that their love and support will always be there for us in our life ahead. I reserve my last comment for Natalie. You have many qualities which cause me to love you. But one, which I hope we both share, will help us through life together and that is the ability to laugh in most situations and the ability to laugh at ourselves first and foremost. Hand in hand, with laughter in our hearts, we face life together.*'

Andy, taking up the cue, struck the right note when he gave a perfect example of the laughter - sometimes manic laughter - that characterised our family life when he said:

'*As a practical joker, Des never quite knew when enough was enough.*

Picture the scene. It is fairly late at night. Derek has been out. Mum and Dad breathe a sigh of relief that he is home. What is it with parents? I mean, 21 and they still shout, 'Is that you, Des?' I mean, they had spoken to me five minutes ago so it's either Des or Jack the Ripper. Having ascertained it is Des, they then proceed to drift back to sleep. The sound of their voices, however, has let Des know that they are still awake, just awake. He is certainly awake and, as always, ready for mayhem. Imagine with me, if you can, the scene from the parental bed as they hear the sound of the door opening. There, silhouetted against the light, stands a figure with a gun in hand. A big gun... A super-duper water-blasting gun. A gun with 100 per cent drenching possibilities. But no one in their right mind would use it.

The figure stands motionless, finger tensing on the trigger. Dad attempts some negotiation. The fixed expression on Des's face reveals the sad fact that the light is on but no-one is at home. He jumps Rambo style to a shooting position and the duvet offers no protection.

The next few moments are pure comedy. Mum locks herself in the loo and Dad heads for the front door, which Des quickly locks on his departure. Parishioners, coming from the nearby Black Bull find it strange the minister is locked out of his house, water dripping from him as he stands in a pair of Y fronts.

Life at number 1 Glebe Gardens was always fun. Sometimes manic but always fun. Laughter was a fairly steady ingredient in our lives together.'

And that pretty well summed it up.

Joan and I have been enormously blessed by two good sons. We have been equally blessed by their choice of wives and the icing on the cake has been Ben, Josh, Rowan and Jake. All different, all unique. To each of them, in the very early stages of their lives, as I lay beside them on the carpet, and much to their parents' amusement, I said the same thing: 'Do you like me?' Then when they did not answer, I whispered in each of their ears, 'I liked you the first time I saw you.' And I did.

In the summer of 2013, life took a sobering turn for both of us. Joan began to complain about a lump in her neck. 'It's nothing,' she would say. Eventually she did decide to seek medical advice and after a battery of tests and investigations, a tonsillar cancer was diagnosed. She embarked on a punishing regime of radiotherapy and chemotherapy, the object of which was a cure.

Having often been openly critical at private meetings and public meetings with the Health Board, I have to say that the level of care she received was awesome. Ms Fiona MacGregor, her surgeon, was reassuring, kindly, compassionate and just inspired within us a feeling of confidence. It is said by some, 'Surgeons do not often exude personality and charm.' I do not believe that to be true. What I do know is that Fiona MacGregor was the antithesis of such a stereotype. She was ably supported by her clinical nurse Lesley Sabey, a charming girl. Joan and Lesley found they had mutual friends and a shared love of dogs. At all times the level of care and concern was second to none.

On 26th December 2013, Joan embarked on a debilitating 6 weeks course of radiotherapy. So from Monday to Friday we would leave Alexandria, bound for the radiology unit at the Beatson for her 9am (or thereabouts) appointment. Strangely enough, a sort of camaraderie developed among the fellow sufferers and it was not without humour. There were also two courses of chemo, which took the feet from Joan and she spent some time in ward B1 under the care of another Vale Lass...Fiona Thomson (Maybe it helped that I had married her!!!) .

Into our lives at this dark time came Frances Campbell, again a lead clinical nurse dealing with head and neck cancers. During a consultation with Joan at her lowest, physically and mentally, Frances leaned over, took her hand and just said, 'What are we doing to you?' It was one of those transcendent moments where a light shines in the darkest hour. Married man though I am, and married woman though she is, at that moment I think part of me fell in love with Frances Campbell.

It is often tritely said, 'It's a small world'. But it is. A few weeks down the line, when Joan was again back in hospital, I received a text from her that said, 'Do you know who Frances is? She is John Kelly's daughter'.

What a remarkable piece of news. John was my buddy at the Vale Hospital, always there if I needed advice when I was involved with the hospital board. That night I phoned John and Rosemary and said simply, 'John, Joan is in the Beatson. I prayed we might be spared this but God did not answer my prayer. What he did do was send an angel, and that angel is your daughter.' There was silence. 'John are you there?' I said.

'I cannot speak,' he said. Emotion had taken over but there was a man so proud of his daughter.

On 6th February the treatment was over and there was a very long slow climb back to what Joan had been before the illness. It was not easy and there were setbacks, but two years later she is back to the lass I knew.

We were engaged in Kilbarchan West Church on Christmas Eve at the stroke of midnight in 1968. Christmas Eve 2014 - 46 years later - found me conducting the watch night service at Old Kilpatrick Church, where I had been acting as locum during their vacancy. Joan was edging back to good health. The congregation knew her story.

I surprised her again - and indeed surprised the whole congregation that night - by walking down the aisle on the stroke of midnight saying that Christmas was a time for giving and that I had in my hand a gift I wished to present to my wife. It was an eternity ring – she deserved it for putting up with me for all those years.

Joan had slipped into the church (incognito) with our friend and my former secretary at Bonhill, Alice McWilliam, who in a loud voice let it be known, in case there was any doubt, 'I'm not his wife.'

Jesus once said, 'Don't worry about tomorrow, tomorrow will take care of itself.' Or, as Lena Martell would sing, 'One day at a time.' I think Joan taught me that lesson. Today is all we have got.

CHAPTER ELEVEN

THE EPILOGUE

In retrospect, I realise my life has been built on three pillars: Family, Friends and Faith. I have dealt with the first two. Now let me close with the last.

Years ago, at school, I read a poem by Walter De La Mare called *The Traveller*. I don't know why, but it caught my childish imagination. The poem tells of the traveller knocking at the door of a deserted forest mansion. The crushing silence of the scene is disturbed by the traveller hammering on the door.

"Is there anyone there?" he asks. There is no answer and yet as the silence, disturbed by his actions, surges back he is left with the overpowering feeling that there is someone there. There is some other unseen presence.

Is anybody there? To find an answer, people have looked to the heavens. They have stood in the silence and asked, 'Is there a God? And if there is, where is he?' Those questions have led to many answers. Some have concluded there is no way we can know.

Jean Paul Richter wrote *I have travelled the world; I have risen to the stars. There is no God! I have gazed into the gulf and cried out, 'Where art Thou?' And no answer came. We are alone.*

Others have concluded there is a God, but a God so remote and uninterested he has forgotten us. Mark Twain wrote, *God doesn't know where we are and wouldn't care if He did.*

I suspect that there are times when even churchgoers wonder the same thing. In spite of the hymns they sing...in spite of the prayers they say, there are times when God just does not seem to be around. Pope

Julian knew this feeling when he said, *When I pray, God seems to be deaf.*

There have been times when I have been with the parents of a child who has died, or I have sat with families as illness has claimed the life of one they loved. I understand the agony and grief that produces these questions. We are hurting, we are grieving. And, like the traveller in the poem, we want to know, 'Is anybody there?'

The Bible does not make much of an effort to prove that God exists. Indeed, the first verse begins with the assumption that God is there. It says, *In the beginning, God...* The Bible simply begins with what it believes to be the obvious.

We cannot prove God; we cannot put God in a test tube. It is the same with love. You cannot prove love. Love is represented by what you do, by what you say and by how you live. And so it is with God. The Bible assumes the obvious, that *God is...*

However, I would maintain, that we can see God. We can see God in the steady, unfailing order of creation. Every day the sun shines and every night the stars twinkle. There is order around us. When we look at the universe in all its magnitude and the atom in all of its infinitesimal perfection, we begin to grasp the greatness of God in creation.

Some years ago a computer so precise and accurate told our scientists we needed periodically to add one second to the year. Indeed, since 1972.... 26 seconds have been added, the last one on 30th June 2015.. How did the computer know? The answer is simple. The computer tested itself against another clock - the universe itself.

When Jesus preached, he often used the world around him to make the point of God's presence. He said no flower ever bloomed that was not nourished by God's care. He said no sparrow ever fell to the ground without God being aware. He said that God knows so much about you and me that even the hairs of our head are numbered. For some of us, God does not have too much numbering to do!

Some things we take for granted. Maybe constancy dims our gratitude. Because the sun shines each day, we scarcely notice it;

because the seasons come with regularity - spring, summer, autumn and winter - we accept it. We tend to look for God in the spectacular and miss him in the ordinary.

God is among us, working and moving in our midst. God is not an absentee landlord. I believe He is in all our efforts to bring light out of darkness, in every act of compassion, every act of mercy.

God is in our hospitals where the staff care for those who are sick. God is in the work of those organisations, like Christian Aid or Amnesty International, that fight for peace and justice and fairness. God is there where kindness and forgiveness are shown; I believe there is something at work in history that is beyond us, and that the destiny of the world is in better hands than ours.

However, I also believe we see Him in Jesus. Look to the one who showed what God is like by what he said and how he lived. Think of the influence he has had. An anonymous poem says:

Twenty centuries have come and gone,
All of the armies that ever marched,
All of the navies that ever sailed,
All of the parliaments that ever sat,
And all of the kings that ever reigned,
Have not affected the life of man on this earth
as much as that one solitary life.

I also believe God speaks to us through the Bible - speaking to folk like us, ordinary folk, flawed folk, about His plan and purpose.

In my ministry, there have been times when I've wondered just where God has been; but there have been many more times when I have felt a guiding hand when I have felt inadequate to the task I've felt called to perform.

God speaks in life's experiences and often through others.

Calum phoned me and asked if I would visit him in hospital. He had attended Bonhill Primary with Andrew. He was a bright pupil, who later went on to Keil School in Dumbarton where he excelled academically. After University, he pursued a successful career in journalism but then changed careers to study law.

Sadly, in his early thirties, life was slipping away from him. I journeyed to Glasgow with a heavy heart, struggling to know what I might say. I entered the room where he was being treated. He rose, moved towards me, and we hugged. Later we began to talk. He told me he and his partner had entered into a civil partnership. He then said, looking at me with those bright intelligent eyes, 'I wanted to ask you to say a little prayer at the ceremony but I would not compromise you.'

At that moment, I could not speak, and eventually managed, through tears, to say very simply, 'Calum, if you had asked I would have said yes.'

Perhaps some of my colleagues would find that odd. So often in the New Testament you read the words 'And Jesus had compassion on them.' He cared - he would have cared for Calum, of that I was sure. That precious, heart-rending moment has influenced my thinking in ways Calum could not have imagined. I believe God spoke to me through Calum.

Sitting in Ford's theatre in Washington DC, the place where US President Abe Lincoln was assassinated, I watched a play entitled, *All I Ever Needed to Know I Learned in Kindergarten*. A silly title in many ways, and a definite lie, but I was intrigued and soon captivated; and, more to the point, made to think. What do you learn in nursery school? You learn the simple things like sharing, not hitting others, playing fair, clearing up the mess you have made, not taking things that don't belong to you, saying sorry if you have hurt someone. To say nothing of washing your hands before you eat, holding hands in traffic, sticking together. As I watched the play, I thought maybe there *was* truth in the title.

Then there was a sketch with a young fellow and an old chap. They were employees in a hotel and the young fellow was complaining about his working conditions. Indeed, he had a long litany of complaints.

Meanwhile the old fellow sat silently. The young fellow concluded by complaining about the lack of variety with the food –'Every day it's sauerkraut and wieners [sausages].'

The old chap then said, 'I spent months in a concentration camp when we longed for sauerkraut and wieners. The problem with you, young man, is you do not know the difference between an irritation and a problem. A lump in your porridge is an irritation. A lump on your breast is a problem.'

I thought of all the times I had made an issue of an irritation while others were dealing with a problem. Maybe God was giving me a nudge.

Joan was never one for cruising on any ocean liner, but I persuaded her. I remember well, as we walked towards the ship berthed at the port of Civitavecchia - the port for Rome – her looking at the towering vessel and saying, 'If that moves from side to side, in any way, I am off it.'

I said nothing. Sometimes a husband knows just when to keep silent. Thankfully, it did not move - and she loved it.

The big plus about this particular cruise was that it was scheduled to visit Israel. It allowed us to visit Jerusalem, Bethlehem, Masada, Nazareth and the Lake of Galilee. It was strange walking where Jesus must have walked.

We all look at the great sights of the world - whether the wonders of nature or of human ingenuity, or the sites that have inspired people to faith - and we all feel differently about them. However, there was something strangely moving about standing where Jesus may have been crucified. I stood in silence. Likewise when I walked among the ancient olive trees in Gethsemane, looking up towards the walls of Jerusalem. I thought of the seven days that Christians call Holy Week and of how those seven days changed the world.

Then to Bethlehem. It was dark when we got there. Standing on Manger Square, I looked towards the darkness of the hills where the shepherds must have sat and looked towards the lights of that 'little town'. Was that how it was?

My reverie, however, was interrupted by a wee lad who stood beside me and asked, 'Do you want to buy a camel?'

This offer was full of possibilities. I could have cut a fine figure astride a camel going along Main Street in Bonhill. If the Rev Allan G Hasson could ride a white horse, then the Rev Ian H Miller would go one better with his camel.

Before entering a bartering situation, which might have involved Joan as a 'trade-in', I saw what the little lad had in his hand. It was a tiny camel made out of cedar wood. Of course I would buy it. The price? Well it seemed that wherever you went the price was the same -- '*Only one DOLLA'!*'

I took his camel and paid the 'dolla', then said, 'Come onto the tour bus and sell your camels.' He told me he would not be allowed, so I took his camels and went onto the bus and sold 20, which was his entire stock.

I can still see his face and big brown eyes as he waved to me, his new Western friend. I often wonder about him. Is he still alive? Has he been caught up in the strife and sadness of that country?

The other thing that impressed us was the fortress of Masada. It looks much like any other mountain in the desert but it was on that mountain that Herod the Great built a fortress. And it was there that a group of besieged Jews defied the Roman Army. For three years, they managed to hold off 10,000 troops who had every modern weapon at their disposal. Initially they tried starving the rebels out, but when that failed, they constructed a huge ramp to reach the wall. They then dragged a battering ram up the slope and gained entry. When it became obvious that the end was near the Jewish leader called upon his followers to die as free men and women rather than face capture. They took their own lives.

On that same day, we visited the Dead Sea. It was an experience. You are told you cannot sink in the water but somehow you do not quite believe it. As you walk out into the sea, your body just lifts up. You can lie on your back and read the news as easily as if you were on a deck chair. You just have to watch the pages do not get wet.

*

There is little doubt that the Church does not have the influence it had 100 years ago, or even 40 years ago. Yet I still believe it has a contribution to make, and maybe that contribution can be best made at a local level. In her Christmas Message of 2015, the Queen quoted a few lines from John's gospel: *...the light shines in the darkness and the darkness has not put it out.* The influence of Christianity has been positive. I have had enough of those who try to denigrate the Christian faith and suggest it has a negative influence on society. I have some sympathy with the National Secular Society's desire to separate Church and State. Often I have felt that the relationship is too close, even too cosy to the "establishment" I have a problem, however, with the aggressiveness of some of their supporters who denigrate the Christian Faith and suggest that it has a negative influence on society.   I am aware of the increasing number of funerals taken by humanist celebrants and have no issue with them when that is the wish of the deceased or their families. Sometimes, however, it comes to a point when families feel awkward about approaching the Church when they may not have entered its doors for years. At times like those, the Church and its representatives must be seen to be open, affirming and non-judgemental.

I *do* have a problem with hard-line secularists. If there is no God, if we are not His children, what are we, a mere bundle of cells? Richard Dawkins' world is not a world I want to live in. Those who reject God have always believed we can make the world a better place without him. I ask if people were freer in Godless, communist Russia. Was Stalin a humanitarian? Is Mugabe? Would you see China or North Korea as places where human life is highly regarded or people are allowed freedom of belief? In our country, it was Christian people who fought for the abolition of slavery and in America the Church was prominent in the Civil Rights movement.

I would contend that most of the great philanthropists and humanitarians in history were motivated by faith. What we take for granted today has been made possible by the men and women of faith in the past who fought for it. I am proud of that.

In the Vale of Leven, the first education and hospital provision was Church-inspired; add to that the provision of a lending library, a benevolent fund, leisure facilities and meeting places.

Was it militant atheists who were moved to tears in Bonhill Church by the young people of Preparation for Life, or sent boxes to Albania, or arranged concerts for Haiti? Many years ago, Tony Stewart drove a lorry load of goods from the Vale directly to the good people of Poland, simply motivated by faith. I could go on and on. I believe that there is no better rule of life than the rule that Jesus gave us - 'Love God, and love your neighbour as yourself.' I will wait for militant atheism to come up with a better rule. I will not be holding my breath.

Though my faith has never faltered, sometimes my faith in the institution of the Church falters. We all fall short of the pattern set by Jesus Christ. Now we are marginalised, no one bothers too much what the Church has to say. However, I wonder if, for years, we have sat too cosily with the establishment, reluctant to criticise or speak out.

In our area, the Church would take a view on school closures, health issues, poverty and the nuclear issue. These things would be debated at a local level and at the General Assembly. Such debates were often fiery and full of passion on both sides. Today it seems we are more likely to be worked up about same sex relationships than the renewal of Trident.

Someone once said, 'I care less about the sins committed in the bedroom, rather more about the sins that are committed outside it.' Sometimes it seems that the Church is scared of taking a risk. If the men that Jesus called had not taken a risk, leaving their livelihood and setting out on a grand adventure, the Christian Church would not exist today. We have become too comfortable, happy not to rock the boat.

I have often been accused of trying to please everyone and that is probably true. I hate conflict and hate to cause offence. Yet I also know that sometimes my strongly-voiced opinions have run the risk of alienating folk I know and respect. The referendum would be the classic case of this. I was firmly in the Yes campaign. In fairness, for me, it was a 'no brainer'. As an ardent anti-nuclear campaigner, I embraced the vision that one day Scotland could be nuclear free. I, along with 33 other Church ministers, signed a declaration supporting independence, which appeared in *The Herald*. People felt very strongly about the issue and yet remarkably I do not think the dire prophecies of friendships being irreparably damaged ever came to pass. Indeed, our country should be very proud of the fact that the issue, which did arouse passion and strong opinion on both sides of the debate, never really boiled over. There were some minor skirmishes, but not the violence often seen in other countries when such major issues are debated. Well done Scotland!

I have been privileged to work with some fine colleagues - some who have even gone on to greatness. Three of them became Moderators of the Church of Scotland - John Chalmers, John Cairns and John Christie. I wonder if their initials - JC - had anything to do with it. Good guys every one. However, sadly, among the clergy there are the pompous ones, those who forget that Jesus called them to 'wash feet'. Humility and Ministry or Priesthood should go hand in hand. I am not convinced it always does.

The Vale of Leven has always had a great musical tradition. It amuses me to think that just over 100 years ago, when the choir met to practice the psalms (they did not sing hymns then) they did not sing the 'Holy' words. Instead, they sung doggerel. The 'Holy' words were only for Sunday. Can you imagine those rather dour Presbyterians, with solemn faces, singing this in four-part harmony, perhaps even to the tune Crimmond?

As I was looking up the lum,
The bright sky to behold,
A lump of soot came doon the lum
And made me quite blindfold. AAAAAAAAMEN!

Yet there is a serious side to this. The 'Holy' words were just for a Sunday. From this may we deduce that somehow your attitudes and behaviours were expected to be different on a Sunday. I believe whatever your faith, your beliefs, your values, those things that you live by and hold to be true should be 24/7. You should not put them on and take them off like a suit of clothes. You live by them and stand by them. For me, the ministry was very much like that. However imperfectly at times, I hope I tried to be there for congregation and parish 24/7; and, in retirement, to the best of my ability, and as long as health allows, I will continue to be there.

In 1225, some monks came from Paisley Abbey. They sailed down the River Cart then up the Clyde, turning into the River Leven before making their way upstream. They had been granted the rights to fish for salmon in the Linnbrane Pool, locally known as the Chapel Hole. It may have been fishing that brought them, but somewhere along the way, their target changed. Maybe it moved from salmon to sole, or souls. They became, in the words of Jesus, *'fishers of men'*.

It has been a privilege to follow in their footsteps. Early records from the time of the monks until 1458 are patchy, but from that date until now, we have a record of the 36 clergy who have served the parish of Bonhill. I am proud to say I have been the second-longest-serving of that number.

Just over 100 years ago, General Booth, founder of the Salvation Army, entered the Royal Albert Hall to give his last, most notable address to a packed crowd of 7,000 Salvationists. Those words sum up the essence of ministry:

'While women weep, as they do now, I'll fight; while children go hungry, as they do now, I'll fight; while men go to prison, in and out, in and out, as they do now, I'll fight; while there is a poor lost girl upon the streets, while there remains one dark soul without the light of God, I'll fight, I'll fight to the very end!'

Things have changed since Booth's day, but wrongs, inequalities, and injustices remain; the rich get richer, the poor poorer. Some children, due to circumstances over which they have no control, are doomed from birth. Young people who have worked and studied hard find it difficult to find meaningful employment. We spend billions of pounds on weapons of mass destruction while our National Health Service creaks. Women and children still live in fear of violence. People face discrimination because of their religion, colour, creed or sexual preference.

In these difficult days - when political leadership is suspect and moral leadership is weak, when to stand up for the kind of values that this nation has taken for granted, but now questions, is difficult - I believe, as a Christian, that it behoves us even more to speak with courage and conviction.

My friend, Iain Galbraith, said to me shortly after my 'retirement', 'Your work is not done.' I believe he may be right.

OTHER TITLES RECOMMENDED BY NEETAH BOOKS

All these titles can be found and ordered at discount and signed on the Neetah Books website – www.neetahbooks.com

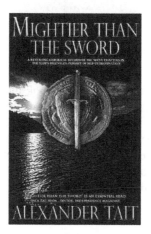

Mightier than the Sword - by Alexander Tait, is a book about Scottish nationhood. It tells the dramatic story of William Wallace, the greatest warrior and martyr for Scotland s ancient liberty. It uncovers the fascinating history of the symbol which has for over 700 years represented the nation s heroic struggle for freedom. It provides a revealing record of the many chapters in the Scots relentless pursuit of self-determination, and, through the personal experience of the author, it illuminates what Scottish nationalism means in our own era. In September of this year, 2014, the Scots will decide democratically whether to remain within the 300-year-old union with England, or to re-join the community of nations as an independent state. For those who would understand the historical and emotional forces, the grievances and the vision, behind the independence campaign, Mightier than the Sword is an essential read. "Mightier than the Sword" is an essential read - Jack Paterson, Editor, Independence magazine.

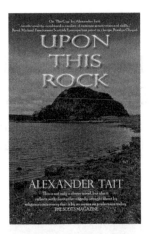

Upon this Rock - by Alexander Tait. This book has it all, romance, subterfuge, and adventure. It is set amidst an important era of Scottish history and manages to both educate and excite. It is a book that every church goer should read. It is especially relevant in an age where religious bigotry still raises its head. Apart from being a thoroughly good read it is also an attempt to sensitively look at the Reformation against the broad sweep of Scottish history. As befits all good books the ending is especially worth waiting for !!!

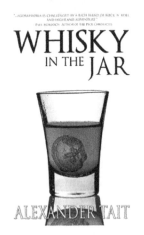

Whisky in the Jar - by Alexander Tait, is an historical novel based on the illicit whisky distilling and smuggling activities that occurred around the eighteenth century on Loch Lomondside. Duncan Robertson is an heroic figure who finds himself ensnared in the conflict between the Highland people and the British military a generation after Culloden. It is also the story of the man who writes the novel. A man fighting his own battle against the mental oppression of agoraphobia, alcohol dependency and the threat of job loss. Where Duncan Robertson's weapons are the broadsword and the pistol, the author uses rock 'n' roll and eastern mysticism. These themes are as vibrantly interwoven as any Highland tartan, with richly colourful characters, romance, suspense and dry Scots humour.

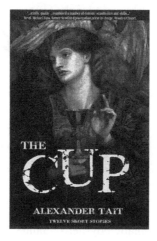

The Cup – by Alexander Tait. In this richly varied collection of a dozen short stories, Alexander Tait draws from his skills of imagination and historical research to enable his readers to encounter Rock legends of the 'sixties, the court of King Arthur and a Roman centurion on the shores of Loch Lomond. Tait's characters are to be found on the Arctic Convoys, the beaches of Dunkirk, Blitz-torn Birmingham and the surface of the Moon. They have been crafted with understanding, warmth and humour, and demonstrate the great truth - that it is in the lives of the ordinary that the extraordinary is to be found. The tales, which range in time from the Crucifixion of Christ to the present day, all deal in their different ways with the eternal battle, within individuals and nations, between good and evil.

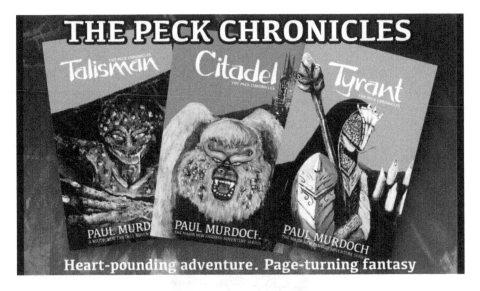

THE PECK CHRONICLES

Talisman   Citadel   Tyrant

PAUL MURDOCH

Heart-pounding adventure. Page-turning fantasy

The Peck Chronicles – by Paul Murdoch. Talisman, Citadel and Tyrant are the first of a seven-book series. Inspired by the area around Alexandria and Loch Lomond, they feature an asthmatic boy-hero – James Peck and his crazy friends as they battle monsters and magic in an effort to save their families and several planets along the way. "A fantastic adventure series for 'children', 9-90yrs. Pratchett meets Tolkien…with Balloch [and Alexandria] clearly recognisable in the landscape." – Keith Charters, children's author.

Talisman

James stands on a hillside, staring at a massive, three-toed footprint… and the crushed animal within it. Is the print a link to the unexplained disappearance of his father?

Within hours James meets Mendel, a wizard from another world – Denthan – who is trapped in a body that is not his own. Soon they do a deal. James will help Mendel back to Denthan before disaster befalls it; in return, Mendel will help James search for his father.

But Denthan is full of monsters. And it is about to be consumed by a battle for supremacy…and survival. If James is to save Denthan – and his family – he must locate a powerful talisman. Except that not even Mendel knows what it looks like.

Citadel

The Hedra wizard Dendralon sees the impending destruction of Denthan as an opportunity to increase his power.

Intent on stopping him, James Peck needs to journey to the Eden Tree, deep in the Forest of Eldane.

If he can find the goldfish-wizard Mendel and use the Talisman, there may be a chance to stop Dendralon.

Eldane is full of danger, including Mertols and giant Trolls. Right now, though, James has to focus on his mortally-wounded best friend Craig … and on finding his own father before it is too late.

Can he save those closest to him and save Denthan from Dendralon's evil?

Tyrant

The odds are stacked heavily against James Peck and the wizard-goldfish Mendel. One year on from their extraordinary Denthan adventure, the zany villagers of Drumfintley find themselves the last line of defence against an invasion of Earth.

The scale of the threat becomes clear when a whole new array of monsters and dark magic begins to emerge from Loch Echty's murky waters. Mendel suspects his oldest and greatest foe – the Tyrant.

Beneath the Loch, Mendel and James discover the submerged village of Fintley. Can its presence explain what is happening? They may not be around long enough to find out, as they are targeted by assassins.

With the survival of humanity at stake, family ties and friendships are about to be tested to the limit in this epic new setting.

The Tiffy & Toffy Picture-book Series – by Paul Murdoch

Tiffy and Toffy – The Squashed Worm and Bramble Pie
Tiffy and Toffy – The Big Red Monster
Tiffy and Toffy – Annie Adder's Gold
Tiffy and Toffy – The Great Vole Rescue
Tiffy and Toffy – The Lucky Pellet

These colourful picture-books are brilliant for young children 3- 7yrs who love animals and adventure. There are items to find and count, hidden in the pages. The books have been used all over the world to help children with English and counting. (Used by UNICEF, Asthma UK, East Bali Poverty Project and Glasgow – The Caring City Charity)

Coming soon: **Sunny** – by Paul Murdoch. Racial prejudice and sectarianism come to the surface in a small Scottish town during the 1970's as Sunny Wilson tries to break through his school mates' narrow views and solve the mystery of a fatal crash.

Paul performs children's workshops all over the world in schools, libraries and at festivals. For more info, go to: www.paulmurdoch.co.uk

ning Source UK Ltd.
n Keynes UK
V06f1823070616
332UK00016B/346/P